Active Leadership:

A Blueprint for Succeeding and Making a Difference

Active
Leadership

H Lloyd Publishing

An electronic version of this book is available at Amazon and other online retailers

ISBN: 978-0-9835974-9-0

Also by Hodges L. Golson

Influence for Impact:
Increasing Your Effectiveness in Your Organization

Thanks, Mom and Dad.

Contents

Introduction

Do you want to be a successful leader? Then hire smart people who get along well with others, who do what they're supposed to do, and who work hard. Set a great example, and reward the right behavior. Simple concepts: difficult execution.

Not everybody wants to be top dog: and that's fine and fortunate, but if you work in an organization, much of your life depends on what the top dog does, so you need to understand the world in which he or she lives.

Some of this material is based on academic research. The rest is the result of practical observations and insights, gained over the course of a career in assessing, coaching, and consulting with top executives in some of the most successful organizations in the world.

This is a practical roadmap of useful insights for anyone who works in organizations, especially those who must lead and manage. If you use these guidelines actively, you'll be a more successful leader at any level. Leadership, however, is not about mechanically following a set of instructions to get people to do what you want. It's about getting people to *want* to follow you. That's more about who you are. And how you behave ultimately determines who you are. This blueprint describes the behavior of successful leaders and highlights some of the important concepts to consider in your leadership journey. It presents some of the realities you face, with practical suggestions for succeeding, and staying effective, in any leadership role.

ONE

Life's tough: life at the top isn't always easier

John decided early in his career that he wanted to run an organization, or at least to be one of the senior decision-makers. Through a combination of diligent study, hard work, business acumen, interpersonal skill, and sometimes more than a little luck, he finds himself with a seat at the table quicker than he anticipated. He realizes that the top spot might not be in the cards, due to the relative youth of his CEO boss and his own runway. As his limo driver skillfully navigates around various bottlenecks on the way to the airport, he has a rare chance for reflection. Having just been instrumental in highly successful negotiations that will have a major positive impact on the company, he allows himself to feel a justly deserved sense of pride and accomplishment about his career. In reality, he is further along than he ever expected to be, and it's nice to know that his family will be comfortable and secure no matter what might happen to him now. He enjoys his work and his life. With the maturity and insight that comes from successes and failures, he rarely has those Peggy Lee "Is That All There Is?" moments anymore; but still remembers some of the not-necessarily-pleasant surprises he encountered soon after his "arrival" as a senior leadership team executive.

Unexpected consequences

If you want to become a top executive, it might be nice to know what it's like in that role before you get there. Forewarned is forearmed.

Most executives are too busy trying to stay on top of the severe demands of their jobs to think about some of the unanticipated facts and phenomena of life in a key leadership position. Before embarking on this journey, you need to know yourself: your strengths and limitations. And be careful what you wish for. There are real costs to gaining and maintaining power, so look at what life is really like at the top and prepare for it. The following points describe some of the surprises typically hidden from view on the way up.

The executive amplifier

As you move up in an organizational hierarchy, your public organizational life becomes a product of sound bites. You don't have time to build relationships throughout the organization as you move up. People can't get to know you the way they did when they worked directly with you and saw you more often. So they decide what you're like as a person and as a leader by what they see in short, infrequent samples of public behavior. And because what you do now can have a major impact on them, they read a great deal into your words and actions.

If you make an effort to smile and to talk to people, you cultivate the image of being an approachable, concerned, and people-oriented leader. If you show no emotion, people see you as detached, or are likely to project things from their own backstories onto the blank screen you provide. If you scowl, snap at someone, or otherwise look unhappy, they see you as negative, irritable, and unfriendly. It only takes a few times, sometimes just once, for the image to emerge and stick. Company cultures reflect shared values displayed through the behavior of the leaders of the company. Much of a leader's impact on the troops is through the symbolism of his or her behavior, even the little day-to-day things. Success requires managing the optics.

The executive as rock star
The larger your organization and the less often people see you, the more you become like a celebrity. Some people enjoy this, but many are surprised and uncomfortable with it. Few anticipate the demands it places on them, or the downsides of the executive fishbowl. Charismatic rock star executives, who really enjoy this aspect of the role, tend to build personality-based cult followings. This doesn't help the company over the long term. In fact, companies usually suffer in the marketplace after the rock star leader has left.

The executive as energy spark
People look to the leader for their own inspiration and energy. Your job sometimes includes keeping the troops pumped when your own energy and attitude are waning.

Providing the spark for others can drain your own re-sources, especially if you're not a natural extravert. Extraverts typically recharge their batteries by contact with others, while introverts tend to renew their re-sources by having time to themselves.

The cognitive elite

There are plenty of smart people to be found at all levels of most organizations. But, on *average*, executives score higher on standardized tests than do people at lower organizational levels. That's often the reason they're in the executive role – they're good problem-solvers. This is not to imply that any one individual executive is brighter than any one individual from a lower level; but *as a group*, they perform better on measures of general mental ability than people in the supervisory or individual per-former roles.

An unexpected phenomenon that emerges when there are many clever people at the top is the *Apollo effect*, described by psychologist Meredith Belbin from his experiences running large-scale management simulations in the UK and Australia. When he stacked the deck by concentrating a disproportionate number of exceptionally bright people on the same team, expecting them to outperform groups composed of a more random assortment of ability, he found that these "Apollo teams" always under-performed compared to the others. They suffered from too many ideas in these groups, too many clever people to find fault with those ideas, analysis paralysis, and too much intellectual arrogance and competitiveness. He observed that the most effective groups were those with a great deal of heterogeneity and variety in talents, traits, and aptitudes of their members. This is *not* to say that you shouldn't hire smart people (more on that later), but you need to know how to manage them.

The imposter phenomenon

This term was coined by psychologist Pauline Clance, in her book of the same name. It refers to the feelings of inadequacy and guilt many successful people encounter because of, or in spite of, their accomplishments. The internal dialog goes something like, "I'm above average, but not particularly special. I'm not sure I really did anything to deserve being where I am, and I'm worried that people will figure it out. I sometimes feel like an imposter." Most people have occasional feelings of inadequacy, but they derail you in a leadership role if you don't manage them appropriately.

The paradox of feedback

The higher you go, the more you require information and feedback. But the higher you go, the less likely you are to get it. People are inclined to tell executives what they *want* to hear, not what they *need* to hear. They don't get many honest reflections of how they really come across. Issues of power (this woman can fire me), politics (I think he's a lousy leader but he sure responds to flattery), and socialization (kids don't tell Dad what they really think), keep the executive from acquiring good information. In addition, some aspects of the executive personality interfere with the ability to hear bad news. Executives have been reinforced for knowing the answer and being strong in the face of opposition. A good source of unbiased critique is invaluable for a leader's development.

The executive as villain

Many people assume that if you're highly successful, you must have cheated. There is a media and entertainment industry bias against business people, especially those in large corporations. The "greed is good" stereotype colors the lens through which many people view the executive suite, and allows politicians to manipulate public opinion. When a few crooks get caught, the press has a feeding frenzy, reinforcing that narrative. The widely shared bias in academia, entertainment, the media, and government is that if you're in business, you need to be regulated or you'll do bad things. And the "you didn't do this yourself" denigration of success is more widely shared than you may imagine at first. Get used to it.

High visibility but no one to talk to

Lonely-at-the-top is a cliché, but it's true. At each successive level, the peer-group support network becomes progressively weaker. Executive group interactions are not typically characterized by openness and trust. Consequently, there's little opportunity for the executive to relax and receive easy give-and-take interaction, feed-back, and counsel more commonly found at lower organizational levels.

Ambiguous or non-existent reinforcement

At this level, outstanding performance is expected. The bar of expectations is raised with every success. Early in your career, you were recognized for your strong per-formance. Each time you are promoted, however, you're judged by your peers, who were also selected into this faster lane because of their own strong performance. So at each level, you begin to look more and more like the pack. Everybody in the pool is a great swimmer.

You're expected to be successful, so no one's going to notice unless your performance is *not* outstanding. Most top executives and CEOs provide inadequate reinforce-ment and supportive critique as a matter of course. If you don't have a clear set of internal standards, and a pretty good sense of your performance against those standards, you're likely to become anxious in the short haul, and miserable over time in high level roles.

How to fail

Knowing what it's like at the top, to include the potential disappointments, warts, and blemishes, helps prepare you to deal with the difficulties and obstacles you'll encounter. Knowing what *not* to do is sometimes as im-portant as learning what *to* do. This will help you avoid unnecessary heartburn and glitches along the way.

One of the earliest studies of the causes of executive failure was published by psychologists Morgan McCall and Michael Lombardo. They identified a number of fatal flaws that lead to a person's eventual derailment on the way up the organizational ladder. As I recall, their initial research sampled males only. However, this seems equally applicable to women. Listed below are the causes of executive failure they identified.

- Insensitivity to others and abrasiveness
- Coolness, aloofness or arrogance
- Betrayal of trust
- Overly-developed ambition
- Specific business-related performance problems
- Over-managing, resulting in the inability to delegate or to build a team
- The inability to hire good people
- The inability to think strategically
- The inability to adapt to bosses with different styles
- Over-dependence upon advocates or mentors

It might seem odd to start out on a somewhat negative note, but none of this is meant to scare or demoralize you. A realistic job preview is one of the best ways to help ensure a good fit. So if the be-careful-what-you-wish-for message hasn't given you pause, if you're prepared to avoid things that derail people, if you still want to move up in the organization, and if you feel that the rewards of leadership are worth the sacrifices, keep reading. Next are some first-things-first observations to consider.

KEY CONCEPTS

Life in the executive suite can be quite rewarding, but it also has its surprises, not all of which are pleasant. Being in a high visibility position means you must deal with some of the unanticipated and potentially negative side effects of success. You need to be prepared for them and for some of the pitfalls on the way up.

Active Leadership

TWO

Getting there: influence or derail

Sam is an exceptionally competent analyst and team member. He came to the group several years ago with stellar academic credentials and a proven ability to get along with people. He is usually the best problem solver in the group. However, he has seen several peers get promoted recently. He has always had great reviews and encouragement from his managers, so he's having a hard time understanding why people who are far less able appear to be getting quicker opportunities for advancement. He has always assumed that keeping his head down and doing great work will eventually get him recognized. He was taught not to brag or to toot his own horn. And he finds it difficult to ask for things or to draw attention to himself in general. He still feels deep down that his results, his willingness to share and his hard work will be rewarded. But he's also starting to feel overlooked and left behind. He knows he's the best quant in the unit. But he'll have to admit that he would like to have the skills of persuasion he senses in some of his colleagues. On the other hand, he's beginning to wonder if he wants to spend much more time in an organization that rewards such superficiality.

Research and observation indicate that hard skills (quantitative, data-analytical, technical, specialized knowledge) are important for success early in a career;

but that the soft skills (influence, relationship building, and political savoir-faire) are crucial for later success, especially in leadership. People who are rewarded for being the cleverest individual problem solvers tend to assume their good work speaks for them.

We have conducted many thousands of psychological assessments for business clients since our founding as a professional firm over a quarter century ago. This has allowed us to develop an extensive database of scores, profiles, and characteristics of successful high-level people. Analysis of the profiles of several thousand successful people (MBAs from top-tier schools, people in fast-track developmental programs, COOs, CEOs and a wide variety of top executives in general) revealed consistent but rather surprising developmental themes.

The most frequently mentioned suggestions for further growth and development of highly successful people fell into the following two related categories:

- **Influence and persuasion**
  The shortcomings in this category include poor communication skills, tendencies to undersell, marginal self-presentation, introversion, shyness, lack of assertiveness, and so forth.
- **Interpersonal insensitivity**
  The problems here have to do with being too dominant, intense, or impatient; tendencies to push people too hard; excessive competitiveness and a lack of political insight and sensitivity, among others.

If this is true among exceptionally successful people, and among those seen as having high growth potential, the situation is even more acute with people in the ranks, with technologists, and with people early in their career trajectories. Here are two key thoughts to keep in mind for the rest of this discussion:

- **Remember, the world isn't fair and doesn't care about your success.** If you don't learn to increase your base of power, others will – and they won't have your best interests at heart.
- **Brainpower and performance help you to gain power only up to a point.** How you play your cards, and who you develop relationships with, are of equal or greater importance as you get closer to the top.

To be able to influence others, you must have *credibility*. Credibility is a function of two primary factors: *trust* and *expertise*. These are the first two pillars of influence. The first two questions people ask, to decide if you are credible, are: "Do you know your stuff?" and, "Do you have my back?"

In addition to the individual quality of credibility necessary for effective persuasion and influence, the following goals are important to us:

- **Accuracy** – We need to make sense of things, so we

can know whether they present threats or offer advantages.

- **Affiliation** – We want to associate with people we find attractive and helpful. We seek their approval and acceptance.
- **Consistency** – We need to maintain a positive self-image. This makes us strive for consistency, and we'll go to great lengths to *appear* consistent to ourselves and to others.

These pervasive human motivations lead naturally to the fundamental laws of influence. A simple listing of them, however, clearly doesn't do them justice. Books have been written on each of them. These laws are based on a tremendous amount of academic research, but they also can be verified by direct observation.

The Law of Authority
We have a strong drive to seek out higher sources of opinion, direction, and advice. People want to comply with and follow authority. People in positions of authority are seen as credible. If you're not in a position of legitimate hierarchical authority, you should at least project the right image. Dressing similarly to those in power increases the perception of your authority, and we're strongly influenced by people who project optimism, confidence, and a positive attitude. Learn to project power, not only in your speech and mannerisms, but also in your dress. It's a learnable skill. Image be-

comes reality over time. Establish your credentials to emphasize your expertise, or show that a respected and credentialed source agrees with your position. Don't forget, though, that there's no substitute for actually *being* a good source of information and help for others. Over time, this is what establishes a reputation for expertise, not merely the *appearance* of authority.

The Law of Trust

This is one of the two key components of credibility. Once you lose trust, it can never fully be regained. Every time you make a deposit to your trust asset base, it grows; but once you make even a small withdrawal, the entire account is likely to be wiped out. The keys to establishing and maintaining trust are simple, obvious, and often overlooked. They include: always following through; not taking credit where it's not due; never, *ever*, betraying a confidence; never overselling or exaggerating; communicating as fully as possible when you have information that will affect others; and taking the first step by trusting that others will perform as expected.

The Law of Liking

Think of the most credible and persuasive people you know. If you make a list of their traits and characteristics, close to the top will be something to the effect that they are likable. We're strongly influenced by people we like. This means that you need to develop a social network within the context of your work environment. We like people who are similar to us, who make us feel good, who like us, who are optimistic and cheerful, and who are attractive but not perfect. The classic reading in this field is Dale Carnegie's *How to Win Friends and Influence People*. His original principles have been validated by later research, and are for the most part as applicable now as they were 80 years ago.

The Law of Reciprocity

We strive to keep things in balance. If someone does us a favor, no matter how small, we feel obliged, and are likely to help them out in some way. This is a fundamental law that is at the core of our society, but it is also at the foundation of all free market transactions. This is why cultists give you a free flower or keychain on the street, and why charities include holiday stamps or coins with their solicitations. Such "free gifts" dramatically increase donations. We operate by implicit rules of balance and fair play. With apologies to President Kennedy: ask not what this person can do for you, ask what you can do for this person.

The Law of Consistency

We are driven to maintain a positive image of ourselves. To do that, we need to appear consistent to ourselves. This is the basis of the foot-in-the-door technique, and the reason salespeople try to get us to commit publicly that we'll buy a certain item "if they can only find one", before miraculously discovering exactly the model we previously thought was unavailable. Once we commit to a small action or agree with some part of a position, we're much more likely to agree with larger requests or stronger positions in the same direction. We go to great lengths to maintain our self-image of consistency and to reduce the dissonance we feel when we act inconsistently. This is the basis for all rationalization.

The Law of Scarcity

We're strongly attracted to things that are rare, scarce, and limited. Less is more. If we perceive that something might become unavailable, or be in limited supply, its value goes up for us. This is the basis for bidding frenzies at auctions, popular toy shortages at Christmas, speculative investment bubbles, snob appeal, and many other examples of seemingly strange human behavior. We are more strongly motivated to avoid losing something than we are by the chance to gain something.

The Law of Social Comparison

We take our cues about how to think and act from other people. Psychologist Leon Festinger coined the term *social comparison* in his research on the factors involved in attitude change and rationalization. This is a fundamental principle: we're strongly influenced by the groups to which we belong, and by those to which we'd like to belong. We look to others to figure out how we should interpret and respond to new or ambiguous information.

We care what the Joneses think, and about what they do. We stop to look up when we see people in the street looking up. We're more likely to tip the bartender if she's salted the tip jar.

Stanford professor Jeffrey Pfeffer notes that the ability to influence others is crucial to success in a career, and in gaining personal power. His book *Power: Why Some People Have It – and Others Don't* offers useful insights about power in organizations – how to gain it and how to hold on to it once you have it. It's based on real world observation and research, not on theory, abstraction, or political correctness. As such, some of his observations could be at odds with what you see in the popular literature and press. In fact, he warns that most leadership literature can be hazardous to your health, because it doesn't reflect the realities of organizational life.

Some people won't like his observations, but having done a bit of research in this area myself, I see very little to quibble about. Pfeffer makes the case for trying to expand your base of power because many good things come from it, not the least of which are higher levels of physical health and wellbeing. Then there's the money, he notes, not entirely tongue-in-cheek. Listed below are some of the keys to success along the path to power.

- **You need to be noticed,** and need to rise above the organizational noise. Make sure people know about your successes. Find a gap and fill it. Reach out and create something. Don't be afraid to break the rules when you're just starting out – you'll be noticed and thought of as innovative. Don't be stupid about it, though; and if you can define the criteria for success, you'll have the advantage.

- **Be sure you know what success looks like in your boss's eyes ...** and in those of his or her boss.
- **Become adept at some Dale Carnegie skills**, and learn to make people feel good about themselves (it'll make them feel better about you).
- **Flattery works.** Even when people realize you're doing it. What's more, research shows that more flattery works even better. But be careful here. If you're too blatant, you'll develop a reputation as a brown-noser.
- **If you have the chance, pick a department or group with high influence and power**. However, sometimes the path to the top can be found through indirect routes, if you develop your alliances and nodes of information, and if you learn to use them well.
- **Ask for stuff.** We enjoy helping others. It makes us feel powerful, and it flatters to be asked. We also like those we help. This is where the laws of reciprocity and consistency kick in.
- **Networking is important.** It is a learned skill, even if you're painfully shy.
- **Learn to fight** and don't take things personally. Do everything you can to make relationships work, and

to be liked. Sometimes, however, you must simply work effectively with a few people you really dislike. Tolerate and become comfortable with conflict; but don't be a jerk.

- **Get over yourself.** Yes, some of this might sound manipulative, and you could be uncomfortable asking for things directly. In reality, though, people aren't paying much attention to you. They're generally wrapped up in themselves, so don't worry *too* much about how things look. But of course you must protect your reputation for being ethical. You need to build trust for full success, so be careful of anything that could taint your reputation.

- **When you're at the top, stay vigilant.** It's not paranoia – they really *are* after you. But stay humble – you are replaceable, and you need to know when to quit. Hopefully, it will be on your own terms.

All of these principles work, and they all can be misused. If you use them to manipulate or exploit, people quickly figure it out. If people think you're trying to manipulate them, you immediately lose their trust, the absolute cornerstone of credibility.

Although the principles of gaining power can allow manipulative and callous people to rise, those traits are also associated with an eventual loss of power. One of the keys to understanding and dealing with the struggle for power is to lose your misguided faith that this is a just world. The good guys don't always win, and the bad guys sometimes do. Perhaps they often do: but if they've made too many enemies on the way up, even if they bring in their staunch loyalists, people find creative ways to even the score. The world might not be just, but people have long memories and they hold grudges. They like to balance things out however they can. If you don't have much explicit power, you're likely to find underground ways to resist people you don't like or trust.

The core principles of influence – credibility (expertise and trustworthiness) and likability – are important factors that allow a person to hold on to power over time. The most effective leaders realize that power can corrupt even the most well intentioned person, and that you don't get good feedback when you're in a position of power. Effective leadership in a high-level position requires the humility to seek out good data. You never know as much as you think you do – and most of the stuff people tell you is filtered. Even though you might realize they're trying to flatter you, you're still only human and still subject to believing your own good press. So it helps to have people who can give accurate feedback, unvarnished data, and seasoned opinion. That kind of information usually only comes from people who don't have a dog in the fight – people who know you in a different context, who knew you in previous lives, or who aren't inside your organization.

The laws of influence stem from our basic human goals to understand what is happening, to associate with people of value to us, and to see ourselves as consistent. People who understand and use laws of influence appropriately and effectively – without being malicious or manipulative – are likely to be much more successful.

THREE

Getting there: blocking and tackling

Michael is considered smart and visionary. He can see a variety of attractive futures clearly, and usually selects a good path towards their achievement. He enjoys many ideas and explores them in depth. He has the ability to keep his audience spellbound when he describes his various visions and creative solutions. It was no surprise to anyone that he was selected for an operational leadership role in a unit that was stuck in the mud. He approached this turnaround opportunity with a great deal of enthusiasm. Six months later, he's also stuck in the mud. The unit's performance has barely budged, and in some cases even grown worse. This shouldn't have been the case. He came in with a strategy that impressed his bosses and he had many meetings with his own subordinates and several all-hands sessions, to communicate his vision. People seemed to get it and to be on board. However, he is now frustrated by an increasing number of blank stares. Why can they not see his vision? Why can't they just do their jobs and move along the path toward success he has laid out for them? His battle cry was "Together we'll transform this division into the shining star. We can help each other to succeed beyond our dreams." He knows they were excited about it but now it seems they're floundering. Things were so clear at the start. He's beginning to question if his vision for the unit is achievable.

Skills of influence facilitate a successful leadership journey. Some other basics are to be considered, however, not the least of which are those of managing people. This all falls under the heading of "common sense." As a mentor of mine was fond of saying, "There's nothing common about common sense." This is simple and obvious stuff that's easy to overlook when fighting daily skirmishes and obstacles to success in business. Welcome to Management 101.

Succeeding as a leader depends on your ability to select the right kinds of people. We'll talk more about that a bit later. But assuming you've selected or inherited good people, what should you do to lead and manage them effectively? It *should* be easier than influencing those over whom you have no direct control, but that's not necessarily the case. However, if you pay attention to the following ideas, you can make life a little smoother for both you and your people.

Task, People and Self-Management

Ralph Stogdill, one of the earliest leadership researchers, began the first comprehensive studies on leadership effectiveness in the middle of the last century. His work at Ohio State, and that of others later at the University of Michigan, focused on the *behavior* of the leader, rather than the traits necessary for success. Stogdill classified leader behaviors into two broad domains: *initiation of structure*, and *consideration*.

MIT professor Douglas McGregor's *Theory X* (the authoritarian production oriented style), and *Theory Y* (the supportive people oriented style) models were direct reflections of this work. Successful leaders were seen to pay attention to factors related to task success as well as to the needs of the people who must accomplish those tasks. In the 1970's, these factors – task focus balanced by people focus – were popularized by management consultants in successful books and training programs. Robert Blake and Jane Mouton with *The Managerial Grid*, and Paul Hersey and Ken Blanchard with *Situational Leadership*, were the two best known of these.

Some of the key actions and behaviors associated with successful task management (initiation of structure) include setting clear goals, planning, defining metrics, monitoring progress, organizing, delegating, and solving technical problems. Actions associated with success in the people management (consideration) domain include communicating effectively, listening, providing support and encouragement, recognizing and rewarding success, and building and maintaining trust.

In addition to task management and people management, there is a third important dimension of successful leadership. This factor is *self-management*, the macro dimension that enables the proper focus on the other two domains. It enables you to strike the right balance between the two while making sure your personal characteristics and needs don't sabotage things. Insight, and the ability to self-monitor and self-regulate, are crucial to successful self-management. A central component of self-management is self-knowledge. We're all, in reality, three people – the person we believe ourselves to be; the person others believe us to be; and the person we really *are*. You need as much congruence between these three people as possible. Good, accurate sources of feedback are necessary to narrow the gaps and enable appropriate self-management strategies.

Achievement – the fundamental process

My first exposure to work flow analysis was a university class in industrial engineering. The text defined the tasks of the leader as planning, organizing, and controlling. Well, that's generally true, but as anyone who has tried to manage people knows, it's not exactly that crisp. Most of the time, leaders are just trying to hold things together and solve the last unanticipated problem. They usually have little chance to reflect on the process beyond getting through the crisis du jour. However, there is a certain flow of events, which characterizes the accomplishment of work in organizations. This was described by psychologist and leadership behavior researcher Clark Wilson, in his presentation of *Task Cycle Theory*, where work is envisioned as following a generally well-structured cycle of events, from goal setting to celebration of results. Similarly to my original college text, this is a good way to encapsulate and define activities, but doesn't anticipate some of the real world sloppiness and ambiguity people encounter day-to-day. Nevertheless, it is helpful to illustrate key points about how work is accomplished.

The Goal

Your success in getting things done in an organization hinges on one key component – the *goal*. This is the first step in the cycle and is the key to any accomplishment. The cliché that you must know where you're going or you'll end up somewhere else stems from this reality. As computer visionary Alan Kay said, "The best way to predict the future is to invent it."

Winston Churchill also weighed in with "The empires of the future are the empires of the mind." You might invent futures and build empires in your head, but you'll never bring them to reality without setting clear goals.

The most effective goals have several things in common. Consider the following examples.

> *"We intend to become a world-class provider of IT services."*

This is a clear declaration: lofty and perhaps inspiring. But how will you know when you're there? And when do you intend to get there? It demonstrates only the first requirement of an effective goal – that of defining the end result. The lack of defined metrics and time frames, however, clouds the picture. Compare it with President Kennedy's national goal for the space program, articulated in 1961:

"We intend to put a man on the moon by the end of the decade and bring him back safely."

This illustrates all the requirements of an effective organizational goal – it's clear (nothing ambiguous about getting a man on the moon), inspiring (people got behind it and supported it – it was an article of national pride) and it provided a timeframe (end of the decade – it actually happened ahead of schedule). It also had a clear quality component (get the man back safely).

People want the world to make sense; and they need to know what is expected of them. Because of this, the effective leader communicates the overall goal, and the reasons for it, in the clearest and most compelling terms. Our perceptions of reality drive behavior, so be sure your people have good information about that reality. You must communicate the goal, more often than you realize.

After the appropriate goal has been defined, there are several, sometimes overlapping, steps that define the cycle of progress and accomplishment from that point.

The Plan

It's hard to achieve a goal if you don't know how to go about it. A plan for achievement might be implicit and obvious in the case of basic and simple goals, or it could be more elaborate and complex, in the case of strategic organizational goals. But it needs to be there. This is often an iterative process. For instance, the basic strategic goal may be to double the size of the enterprise within three years. In this case, plans are developed for the overall goal, then sub-goals developed from those plans, to help move the company toward the big target. There can be considerable overlap between setting goals and planning for their accomplishment.

The plan must anticipate problems, define likely solutions, incorporate alternatives, define what is needed, and allocate resources. This process may be facilitated by elaborate tools or can be a general roadmap in your head. It offers a chance to explore options and alternatives for goal achievement.

Facilitation: support with measurement

Once a plan is in place, the leader must facilitate the efforts of the team to implement it and to measure progress. Here, the skills of encouragement and discipline are important. Some people experience internal angst about holding others accountable while also trying to support them. The most effective leaders realize that little will be accomplished if people don't have a way to measure their progress, but also that people need more than just yardsticks.

They need to know what's expected (clear goals and methods) and how they're doing (good metrics); and they need the tools for success. These tools include support, coaching and encouragement, feedback and ongoing communication. Here's where Robert Greenleaf's concept of *Servant Leadership* is most readily apparent in observing effective leaders. They act as if they're there to serve and help people get their work done, to make things better and to grow. One of the most effective questions a leader can ask is, "What can I do to help you succeed?"

There must be a balance between demanding and supportive leadership behavior. The overuse of either style leads to problems: too far in the demanding direction leads to a critical and autocratic style. Too much support leads to an overly permissive, laissez-faire leadership pattern.

Staying in control

Despite the importance of the plan noted here, you can't act as if it's etched in stone. Keep in mind President Eisenhower's comment, "Plans are nothing. Planning is everything."

The plan is a roadmap for a changing countryside. It will have to be updated based on data collected as you progress. The better your feedback loops and controls, the better your decisions on processes, systems, and changes of plans will be. If you don't monitor the process with good, data based, metrics, you won't be able to tell if you're off course, or what you should do about it. If you've anticipated the range of options that will be available, they should be incorporated into the system of metrics and controls so you know how you're doing, and so you know what to do if things are not going well.

Of course, any leader must show support and encouragement, but you can't relinquish control. Abdication isn't an option. You have the ultimate responsibility for success, so you need to maintain the ability to make corrections and tweaks to stay on track. This sometimes means making tough decisions to replace team members who aren't up to the task. But it more often means consistently holding people to the standards and expectations of behavior, performance, and progress dictated by the nature of the task, and by the organization. Sometimes the systems and processes just need to be tweaked, sometimes there needs to be a complete overhaul.

A good performance management process makes this easier. If you communicate the expectations and standards for performance on the front end, things go more smoothly. However, not everyone will share your motivation, knowledge, experience, or ability, so you must make sure everyone receives helpful corrective and productive feedback along the way. This is fundamental to managing – communicating what your people are supposed to be doing, giving feedback about how well they're doing it, and providing suggestions for how they can do it better. Enforcing consequences if they consistently fail to meet standards and expectations is also necessary.

Completing

Once you've solved all the problems and achieved your current goal, you need to turn around and set new ones. A few important items require attention, however, in the final stage of successful goal attainment.

First, celebrate it. This is a chance to reinforce good performance and recognize the efforts of the team. People need to feel that their work is important and appreciated. There's no better way to do this than by public and private pats on the back from the boss. This is a great opportunity to strengthen the bonds of the team and to prime them for more successes. Don't squander it.

A second important part of the finishing process is to reflect on what everyone has learned. There should be a process of critique. This helps you to understand what you did right, as well as to analyze what went wrong – or at least what could have gone more smoothly. Make it positive. Avoid the "Yes you made an A, but you *could* have made an A+ if you'd tried just a little harder" syndrome. A "plus-delta" wrap-up often employed by meeting facilitators is helpful: "What went well? What could have gone better?" This final task is often overlooked in the heat of new demands and pressures, but it's a chance for true learning. Don't miss it.

Making allowances

Since you usually don't have the luxury of having everybody undergo a thorough personality assessment on the front end, it's likely to take a while before you fully get to know the differences and subtleties of the individuals upon whom you must depend. Because of this, it's important to spend time with each individual, and observe them in team activities, to fully develop and flesh out your deeper insights about them and their motivations and abilities. First impressions are sometimes accurate, but it's usually a mistake to judge quickly. It's also a mistake to take too long to figure out who you can depend upon. As with so many issues, the leader must walk a fine line and keep a delicate balance here.

Of course, we all know that one size doesn't fit all and that people are driven by an unending variety of needs, motivations and dreams. And they're enabled by unique combinations of aptitudes, personality traits, and experiences. Some are comfortable being told what to do in a stepwise fashion, while others need to figure things out on their own. Some need constant social interaction, while others prefer to work in isolation. Some will slack off as soon as the boss walks around the corner, while some are tougher on themselves than any boss could ever be. You get the picture – people are different and you can't manage everyone the same way. Some things, however, do need to be consistent across the board.

Communication of the goal and plan, helpful feedback and coaching for better performance, holding people accountable and reinforcing the right behavior: these things are inviolable. The leader must be seen as consistent, regardless of the makeup of the troops. Douglas McGregor's *hot stove analogy* is a good metaphor for consistent discipline. A hot stove glows red (everybody knows it's hot and will burn if you touch it). If you do touch it, the consequences are immediate (it burns you as soon as you touch it). And it is universal (it applies to *everybody* who touches it in the same way).

This kind of consistency must be balanced with flexibility. That is, the most effective leaders also make allowances for individual differences in personality, motivation, ability, and background. This is not to say that some people should get special treatment. Leaders are always judged on perceived fairness. However, they are also judged by the efficacy with which they manage and motivate widely varying personalities of individuals in their teams. This is where coaching skills and insights help you achieve the right balance.

KEY CONCEPTS

Without clear and meaningful goals, nothing happens, no matter how interesting the vision may be. People-, task-, and self-management skills are essential to effective leadership. They come into play in all phases of the cycle of results – goal definition, planning, facilitation, measurement, maintaining control, and celebrating success. Not only must you balance these dimensions, though: you must also balance consistency with flexibility.

FOUR

The leader as coach

Amber's job interview went quite well. She received a very attractive offer, which she gladly accepted. Her new position offers greater responsibility, more money, and a much more professional and supportive work environment. The interview process was impressive. It was a full day of panel and one-on-one sessions with people who were obviously trying to make sure her skills were a match for the demands of the job, and that she would be a good culture fit. They were also approachable and encouraging of her questions. In casual conversations at lunch, one of her future coworkers asked about the best boss she ever worked for, which was easily the most thought-provoking question of the day. Her answer was probably not what they expected. The person who came to mind immediately was Amy Collins, her college volleyball coach. None of the ten-plus people she has worked for in any company, starting with her first job, even came close.

Coach, as everyone called her, helped Amber play at a much higher level than she ever thought she could; and she did the same for everyone else on the team. She kept everyone intensely focused on the overall goal of a divisional championship, while also making sure everyone was fully prepared for each game. That the team won the championship was almost secondary to the sheer joy of working with such a dedicated and focused group of teammates, and playing for such an exceptional coach. She always had high standards and quickly let you know if you did not uphold them. She was a tough and relentless taskmaster, but you knew she had your back and you knew she cared. In addition, in spite of her rigid discipline and expectations, she treated each player with respect and with the advice and coaching she needed at any particular point. She was fair to everyone, but her approach with each girl was different, depending on her unique situation, needs and skills. If you were unsure, she helped build confidence. If you got cocky, she quickly brought you down to earth. When things were not going well off the court, she got to the bottom of it, and was always there with willing support. You just knew that if you talked to her, followed her advice, and worked hard, that things would get better. She knew her stuff, you knew that you could trust her and enjoyed being associated with her. She was tough and demanding, but she was also likable and everyone wanted to perform well for her.

Amber still remembers her with love and admiration. She has a good feeling that leadership in her new company will be much better than at her old place, but she knows there will only be one Coach.

Articulating clear organizational goals is crucial to leadership success. However, people don't come in a standard format. We all share certain basic motivations, but all have our own unique individual motives as well. Of course, a basic leadership function is to set the direction and control the process, but effective leaders must do more. They must also find ways to get people to want to follow them. The best way to do that is to be a good coach.

A good coach understands people

The best coaches are great judges of talent. The unique makeup and motivations of each individual player have a subtle but often huge impact on the overall performance of the team. A key to success here is to understand a person's self-concept. Once you know how each person perceives him- or herself, you have a great deal of basic information about how to help them be more successful. If you feel the self-concept is flawed (for instance, if the tendency is to consistently overestimate or underestimate their own ability), your task begins with providing supportive but clear reality checks.

The law of consistency dictates that people work very hard to maintain a consistent self-image. Unfortunately, this applies to negative as well as positive self-images. A good coach needs effective skills of feedback and critique. If the self-image is too far removed from reality, this process could take some time.

Once you understand people, their individual basic self-concept and unique blend of motivations, you can begin to help them work effectively towards the achievement of personal goals within the overall framework of organizational mission. Helping your people set realistic personal growth goals is a cornerstone of good leadership. It not only cements the facilitating relationship, but also builds organizational strength. People not in the active process of growth and development don't add to your bench strength. If your people don't meet their full potential, you are sure to be at a disadvantage when promotional opportunities come your way. You should always seek a successor: ideally, more than one. One of the best measures of leadership effectiveness is how well you develop others for broader and higher roles within the organization.

A good coach balances the team

The same body of research that gave rise to Belbin's observations on *Apollo teams* generated other valuable insights about the composition of effective teams. He found that the best performing teams had a balance of *team roles* in addition to the necessary functional roles. He identified eight such roles that facilitate success. There are the social roles necessary for communication and outreach that enable teamwork; the creative roles that help generate new ideas; the analytical roles that critique these new ideas and facilitate problem-solving; and the operational roles that keep people focused on the task. It's possible for one person to play a variety of roles, but the function of each role needs to be there.

The team must be balanced. Too many people with an analytical mindset results in a team that spins its wheels and over-analyses, resulting in lack of progress. Too many people with a social role orientation can distract the team from problem analysis and execution. Too many creative people will result in an idea overload that can cause the team to lose focus. Work teams need people to fill the necessary organizational functional roles such as finance, operations, sales, engineering, and so forth. However, you may have a group of exceptionally talented people with extensive functional knowledge who still fail to function effectively as a team. This is often due to an imbalance of team roles. A good coach will ensure that a team is composed of people with the appropriate skills for each position. This includes team members with the ability to play the more subtle but necessary team roles, as well as the functional requirements.

A good coach helps define and achieve positive goals

Executive coaches often use a framework for behavior change that helps people set realistic goals. Many of these are variations of the GROW model for problem solving. This process can be applied to a wide range of circumstances, and can be an effective tool for leaders to help their team members reach full potential. The basics of this model are as follows:

G – GOAL

> This defines the desired endpoint. It describes where the person ultimately wants to be. Therefore, the goal must be very clear so that the individual knows when it has been achieved.

R – REALITY

> This is how far away the person is from achieving the goal. It helps clarify the key steps that need to be

taken, to help the person achieve the goal, and can also show how far that individual has come.

O – OBSTACLES and OPTIONS

To be successful, a person must anticipate problems that might block the way. There are always problems and difficulties; otherwise, the person would already be at the finish line. Once the key obstacles have been identified, the options and resources available to deal with them are defined. However, we can't predict everything. We must consider Donald Rumsfeld's "unknown unknowns." That is, some obstacles will be due to random or unknowable events, so alertness and flexibility are crucial to success here.

W – WAY FORWARD

This is the process of development. That is, defining the appropriate action steps identified in the analysis of options and resources that lead the person towards the achievement of the goal.

Goals are essential to personal growth. Executive coaches often incorporate the characteristics of the effective goal into the acronym SMART.

This means the best goals are **S**pecific (clearly defined), **M**easureable (so that you know how you're progressing), **A**ctionable (they're under your control), **R**ealistic (you can achieve them with appropriate effort and resources) and **T**ime-limited (you have a deadline).

Setting goals is the easy part. The real work lies in achieving them. There is an insidious force just waiting to trip us up and derail our best intentions. An enemy inside all of us keeps us from achieving our goals. Whether you're trying to write a book, develop an iPad app, lose 40 pounds, start a new business, or achieve a personal growth objective, you have a built-in adversary that will be fiendishly creative and stubborn in finding ways to keep you from your goal. This enemy, Resistance with a capital R, is described rather frighteningly by novelist and screenwriter Stephen Pressfield, in his quick and feisty little book, *Do the Work*.

Resistance and its allies – self-doubt, procrastination, timidity, perfectionism, narcissism, our own intelligence and even friends and family – are the powerful forces arrayed against us when we're trying to achieve any worthwhile goal. By definition, you're trying to transform something – yourself, a business, a project, the presentation of great thoughts and ideas, or something just as important or personal. This might be a threat to those closest to you, and to your own self-image. The law of consistency can be an ally when we use it for positive influence, but can be an enemy that tries to keep us in our place when we're trying to do something really different.

A great coach helps a team sustain belief in what they are doing. When you're working on a project and trying to accomplish your goals, consider this as your creed. It's your belief in what can be and what will exist beyond the current reality. Closely related allies are passion, the ability to tap into the natural increase in good ideas once you are on your way, and remembering who you love – that is, who you are doing this for.

It helps to remember that Resistance arises as a second force in opposition to the idea. The idea, the passion and the dream come first. Resistance is the inevitable shadow that tries to block out the light from these positive energies. The achievement wants to exist. Resistance wants to snuff it out before it gets started.

Here are some of the steps Pressfield offers to help you succeed, and to help you coach others to do so:

- Begin before you're fully ready. That is, don't spend any more time on research beyond the basics you need to get started.
- Stay primitive. Keep things on the primal, earthy, and emotional plane rather than trying to be too rational at this point.
- Swing for the seats. Keep your sights very high, because it gets you a lot further toward your goal, even if you fail at first.
- Start at the end. Visualize where you want to go, and work backwards from there.
- And always remember that your internal dialogue, your chatter, your "monkey-mind talk" as the Buddhists call it, is nothing more than Resistance.

Hodges L. Golson, Ph.D.

KEY CONCEPTS

Good leadership is good coaching. A good coach understands his/her people, balances the team by making sure
the appropriate skills are in place (functional roles and
team roles) and helps people set positive goals for
growth. And of course a good coach supports people as
they find ways to achieve their goals.

Active Leadership

FIVE

Leading in tough times

Adam has been pleased with his progress and success in a variety of leadership roles over the past few years. His even temperament and low key manner have served him well in the past and, until recently, he thought that they would be of even more value as the company began to encounter rough sledding. There are strong new competitors, rumors of cutbacks, and there was even talk of a potential merger. People are uncertain and consequently are having a hard time focusing on their jobs. He wants to rally the troops, but is becoming unsure about his particular leadership style in this environment. It was a surprise to him when one of his peers confronted him recently with the news that people see him as detached or uninvolved. He knows that's far from the truth, but he doesn't want to come off as insincere or theatrical just to try to get a rise out of his people. The company hasn't been through such tough times since well before he joined, and everyone's feeling the strain. Now that his colleague has made it clear he thinks Adam needs to show more emotion, he's questioning himself. He wants to bring stability to the situation, but it seems that at least some people want a more vocal, emotional approach from their leaders. Perhaps his style isn't what these times need?

A good leader helps people overcome adversity

Growth through pain is a cliché, but it's also true. It's a

tough fact of life that we don't learn much about ourselves or our character in good times. We can't fully discover our strengths and shortcomings without being tested by adversity. How we deal with it, or how we learn to deal with it, is central to who we are – and how credible we can be in leadership roles. In bad times, all eyes are on the leader. How you behave has a tremendous impact on your people. The best thing the captain can do in stormy seas is keep the tiller steady – unless, of course, the ship is headed towards the rocks.

When people are under prolonged periods of stress and strain, predictable and bad things happen. They can become increasingly wary, and tend to interpret each new sign as an indication of more bad things to come. Negative emotions run high and people are more likely to bark at each other and openly display frustration. They become skeptical of the new and the different, and are prone to reject it out of hand. As the stress continues, fatigue sets in and they become even more pessimistic about the future. Relationships suffer as the focus becomes one of staying afloat as a business. Steadiness and insightful coaching are crucial to survival and success in tough times. A stressful environment increases the leader's potential impact. People look to leaders more in hard times, which is partly a product of the ambiguity that adversity creates.

Focusing on the right things
A critical coaching challenge in uncertain times is to

keep people focused on things that are under their control. You might not be able to affect what happens in the stock market, but you sure can reach out to your customers and provide great service. This sense of control helps people manage their stress and allows them to experience small wins that have a buffering effect. It is critical that the leader or coach provide a broader vision of the future, and a sense of direction and purpose. By linking today's actions to a better future, people gain a sense of perspective. By pointing out to an employee how their individual job links to a broader corporate strategy, you give that person a greater sense of purpose and utility. And that provides significant relief from the debilitating effects of stress.

On the people side of the equation, the key responsibility of a leader or coach is communication. Regular, honest, candid, and consistent communication is key. You must be seen as a reliable source of information, even if it means admitting you don't know. Equally important is listening. By understanding people's concerns, leaders can more readily address them and share with them the information and insights that help reduce misunderstandings and fight negative rumors. In tough times, it is critically important to try to create opportunities for positive emotion. While a sense of humor helps, it is also important to celebrate wins, find ways to have fun, and to thank people. Emphasizing strengths, wins, and good news helps redirect people's attention.

A cornerstone of great leadership is taking care of

the troops. Listening and empathy are important, of course, but you also need to be attuned to signs of burnout. Because much is expected of people in a tough economy, they need to find ways to recharge their batteries. Framing challenges people face as developmental opportunities can often help redefine their emotional experience. While few people would wish to go through boot camp again, most recognize the benefit of that challenge. Seeing current circumstances as being tested in the fire tends to make us more resilient. Remember the words of Winston Churchill: "If you're going through hell, keep going."

Naturally, managing the task and managing your people are essential to success in any circumstances; but in tough times, the self-management dimension is critical. You're in the spotlight even more now. You set the tone. If you are positive, confident, and optimistic, your people are likely to behave in the same way. If you display focus and determination, they are likely to follow suit. In stressful circumstances, you need to manage your behavior to bring about greater optimism and more effective action from your people, and help them manage their own attitudes and behaviors towards appropriate outcomes.

It's natural for people to feel powerless and victimized in tough times, so it is important for leaders to help their people shift from the mindset of the passive victim observing things from the sidelines to that of the athlete playing the game. You must keep them focused on the fact that there are always choices available, and that, although the final score cannot always be controlled, they do have control over how they play the game. If we consistently play with integrity, stamina, optimism, and intensity, we usually surprise ourselves. Even if we lose, we can be proud of our performance. Remember, just as panic and despair are infectious, so are energy and enthusiasm. As you look around your organization, remember the words of Gandhi: "Be the change you want to see in the world."

One way to keep people focused on positive action is not to slip into the trap of automatic sympathy. While it makes a person in victim mode feel good to hear such things as, "That's terrible, you must feel awful, they should fix it, poor baby," and other messages of consolation, those are precisely the wrong messages. They imply that the power is *out there*, with those bad people who are doing you wrong, with that evil competitor or that rotten economy.

A more effective way to get and keep the right focus is with statements such as, "Yes, that's tough – what are you going to do about it?" or, "I wish it was different, but it's not – what did you learn from it?" and "I understand you're angry – so how will you avoid this in the future?" These responses imply that the power remains with the individual and that some positive outcome can arise from a tough situation. A key to great leadership in tough times is to help people see reality, and to help them find appropriate ways to deal with it. Keep in mind the words of Carl Rogers: "The facts are always friendly."

Fred Kofman, in his book *Conscious Business,* provides great examples of shifting from the archetype of the victim/observer to that of the athlete/player.

Leaders often need to help their players reframe their current situations, and see things in a different light. This is important: the conditions that conspire to present you with your current set of choices are not always under your control, but the way you respond to them is. Holocaust survivor Viktor Frankl's book *Man's Search for Meaning* describes the experiences that helped him develop these insights, and illustrates this concept quite effectively. You can't imagine much worse circumstances than Auschwitz, where the Nazis had the power over everything in your life, including whether or not you get to keep it. Some people, however, including Frankl, were able to survive their ordeals in the death camps.

Being a neuroscientist and psychiatrist, Frankl was intrigued by the puzzle of what makes some people re-silient and what causes others in similar life-threatening circumstances to succumb. His observation was that, although people in the camps were deprived of choice in all aspects of their lives, those who retained the human dignity of *choosing how to respond* were more likely to survive. Those who gave up and acted as if they had no control, no choices, were more likely to die. This was also illustrated in studies of learned helplessness conducted by Martin Seligman, one of the primary developers of the emerging field of Positive Psychology.

Dogs that were subject to shocks over which they had no control eventually gave up and stopped trying to escape. Even when the doors to their cages were left open, they would lie down and passively accept the shock rather than try to get out. They could escape the shock simply by walking through the open door, but their previous training had not provided them that frame of reference.

Fortunately, most of us never have to endure such traumatic experiences; but we still whine and complain. It's our nature. Still, we can transcend our nature at times by shifting our frame of reference, realizing that we in fact do have more control than we think, and changing the way we act. Similarly, when we change how we think (often leading to the insight that we in fact do have options), we're preparing to change how we respond and behave. The clear lesson of these results and observations is this: how we choose to respond to a situation allows us to transcend even the worst of circumstances.

The right changes in behavior enable us to make things better. We can choose to see things differently as we become more aware of alternatives and we can consequently choose to act differently as we develop the courage to do so.

Thought questions for bad times
How do you begin? If you're in a bad situation, start with

a question: "What am I going to do to make things better?" This implies analyzing your circumstances with an eye towards seeing what can be improved. As you do this, you may begin to see alternatives you might not have considered. This is when you can see opportunities to act differently. You might not have caused your situation, but you always have the choice about how to respond to it. You have more control than you realize. It sounds simplistic, but sometimes the simple solutions are the best. To help your people shift their thinking from being the victim to becoming an active participant, try these questions:

- What will *you* do to make your life better?
- *When* will you do it?
- How will you *measure* your success?
- *How long* before you know whether it's working?
- What will you do if it's *not* working?

KEY CONCEPTS

When people are under stress, they look to leaders for information, direction, and support. If you can help people realize they have more control than they realize, they will be more effective. Re-framing their current negative situation to help them focus on the things that are under their control, and showing them they can find things they can do, will help them get through.

SIX

Transitions: anticipating the demands of new roles and adapting

Catherine has been fiercely competitive and quite successful in everything she has ever tried to do. She was awarded academic and athletic scholarships, and graduated cum laude with a degree in electrical engineering from a major university. People have always assumed she was destined for greatness. The confidence that came from her many successes reinforced that idea in her mind. She was quickly discovered to be the cleverest technical problem solver on the team in her first job. On recommendation of her bosses, she was assigned to bigger and more complex projects whenever the opportunities arose. She thoroughly enjoyed the work and the challenge of dealing with difficult and multifaceted real world engineering problems. She was known to have exacting standards, and to be quite demanding of other team members, but she got along well with people.

Because of her outstanding work, she has recently been promoted to supervise a similar team in another department. Although this was quite a feather in her cap, she was reluctant to give up some of the interesting and exciting engineering problems she found so stimulating and challenging. Now she has a different sort of problem. She is disappointed with the quality of thinking and the general expertise of her new group. Things she had assumed would be in place appear to be severely lacking in this team. She finds herself having to redo their work on a regular basis. Although she is making a valiant effort to bite her tongue, she is rolling her eyes too often. This stuff is really much simpler than the work of her previous group, and she has a hard time understanding why they don't seem to get it. By now, they should know what they're trying to do, and shouldn't need so much help from her. She finds herself wishing she didn't have to worry so much about other people, especially those who seem so slow on the uptake. Perhaps her path to success should not include having to manage – and babysit – people?

You don't need a shrink to tell you change is difficult. There are powerful dialogues and instincts inside all of us that conspire against us. Change involves letting go of something that has been of value, so it automatically triggers our fear of loss. Change can sometimes threaten our self-concept, releasing the previously mentioned forces of the law of consistency. It also involves expenditure of energy, to learn something new and to deal with all of the previously described forces of resistance.

Obviously, as you move up, you need to develop new skills and insights. Although the lessons learned from your previous lives typically work your advantage, they can sometimes work against you. There are certain skills and perspectives one must develop at each new level. Our natural tendencies are to rely too heavily on the knowledge, skills, and behaviors that made us successful in our earlier roles. But if you don't make the necessary adjustments in attitude, behavior and focus, you won't make a smooth transition. For each new level, success demands letting go of something that was previously of value and broadening your perspective.

From individual performer to supervisor of others
Self-management was earlier discussed as one of the three basic tasks of successful leadership (the other two being people and task management). As an individual performer, you are rewarded for being the most knowledgeable, clever, hardworking, and task-focused person you can be. However, when the job involves supervising others, you just don't have as much time as before to invest in all those other areas. Now, the reward comes from helping others to be successful and relying on them for your own success. But it's not easy to shift from actually doing the work to getting it done through other people. You must let go of some of the behaviors and activities that made you successful as an independent worker. You now must develop and apply your knowledge of motivation and behavior. This involves helping people settle conflicts, diagnosing performance problems, coaching them to work more effectively, and holding them accountable. Although you still might be responsible for many of the earlier activities, you have broader and more challenging goals.

This is a very difficult transition for many people, especially those who have a craft, technical, or professional specialty. It's quite natural for them to feel a loss of security by moving to this level. The idea of losing one's technical edge is threatening: especially if that person is unsure about the ability to direct and facilitate the work of others.

From supervisor of individuals to manager of managers

This transition involves retaining and applying everything you've learned as a supervisor, while shifting to a broader focus. The new skills required at this level are not quite as obvious as those necessary for success in the previous job. Assessment and selection of talent become more important. At this point, you are far removed from being able to be involved in individual contributions. Again, this level requires changes in your time allocation. You now need to analyze how to deploy resources most effectively to the various units under your supervision. What's more, you need to help define and clarify boundaries between units to help settle conflicts, to facilitate efficiency and to foster better working relationships among your people.

Coaching becomes more important at this level, because your direct reports probably have very little formal training about their own new roles. They know how to be great individual contributors. After all, if that were not the case, they wouldn't have been considered for promotion. Like Catherine, however, most of them are still wrestling with some of the changes in perspective, values, time allocation, and scope of vision you encountered in your own initial supervisory role. At this level, you can't help people solve problems they encounter as individual contributors. You're just too far away from that particular theater of operations. One of your major tasks in this role is to help others become more comfortable and effective delegating work, rather than trying to do it themselves.

From manager of managers to leader of a function

Depending on the size of your organization, this may be a position reporting directly to the CEO. Developing new ways of communicating becomes increasingly important at this point. There are now at least two layers of management between you and the individual workers. In addition to this, you might be managing departments with which you are totally unfamiliar. You are interpreting new data and judging how well it reflects reality. You must also communicate a clear and consistent message to everyone in the group, to help them understand the mission, values, standards, and goals that are important to the success of the organization.

The leader of a function must learn to understand and appreciate longer-term strategy. This involves understanding the other functions; and how each contributes to the current and future success of the organization. Here, you need to coordinate with your peers to clarify expectations, to facilitate a solid understanding of what each group contributes, and to define the standards, metrics, and criteria for success. Naturally, politics play a role as well: politics are part of every organization, and tend to become more subtle, yet more intense, as one moves up the organizational hierarchy. At this level, you are generally dealing with competent and ambitious peers, and need to develop even more effective negotiation and relationship management skills.

From functional manager to business unit leader

In smaller companies, this is the CEO position. If not, it usually reports to the CEO. In larger companies, it can report to an enterprise manager responsible for several different businesses. This is the P&L level, and here you have a great deal of autonomy and responsibility. In addition to the strategic and cross-functional perspective, now you must consider questions of risk, profit, and long-term results. This is one of the most challenging positions you could ever hold. It requires the ability to maintain a delicate balance of operations, strategy, financial acumen, and ever more complex and subtle communication and political issues. You must learn to be effective making trade-off decisions between the demands of future goals and current operational needs. The time pressures of short-term profit demands add an extra layer of stress.

Full success at this level requires that you understand and value all staff functions, some of which you might have considered adversarial in previous roles. A common mistake here is to overvalue one's previous function, and to let old loyalties, alliances, and relationships cloud the judgment and impartial vision necessary for success at the business unit level. This is especially true if you have been promoted from your previous function inside the business you now lead.

Deeper reflection and analysis become much more important to the success of a business unit leader. This requires a major shift in time allocation. Planning for business success years in the future cannot be done on an ad hoc basis. It requires time for sustained analysis and deep thinking. At this level, you need to be able to connect the dots from a very wide range of sources, and to be comfortable with a broader and more far-reaching horizon. This is a major shift in thinking for most people, and it requires a concentrated effort to carve out the necessary time and space to do so effectively.

This role requires a keen ability to deal with a wide variety of external constituencies. Here, you must develop a good balance between internal and external perspectives and focus. You can't be involved in every internal decision, so you need to be sure you are focusing on the appropriate mission-critical decisions. Now your scope is the organization as a whole: how it relates and responds to customers; the competitive landscape; the changing technological environment; and regulatory realities.

Successful internal leadership at this point relies heavily on clarifying your message, ensuring its appropriate communication, understanding and using the power of symbols, delivering good sound bites for message reinforcement, and making sure that your behavior is consistent with your words. It involves creating and maintaining a culture that will facilitate success. This is a complex task, and it takes time. It involves developing and communicating a clear and compelling vision, and making sure you have the right people to help you achieve it.

KEY CONCEPTS

Relying on the knowledge and skills that made you successful at one level in the organization will not necessarily help you succeed at the next. In fact, if you rely too heavily on them, they can work against you. The successful journey up the food chain involves letting go of some things that have facilitated your progress so far, learning new skills and perspectives, and making sure you allocate your time appropriately.

SEVEN

Developing your organization: the right people

Bob had a successful early career in large account sales, and is now in his second role as leader of a national accounts group. His team sells complex systems integration services to the company's largest customers. Many of his people have technical and engineering degrees. They are usually quite clever in helping their clients solve complex problems; but they are a bit slower than he would like in developing social relationships that lead to greater business development success over time. Last year, he hired Fred, a candidate from outside the organization, to handle a steady client that appeared to have untapped potential for development. Bob realized that Fred might be a little light on the technical side, but assumed that his winning smile and great social skills would compensate and help him develop the business. As anticipated, everyone responded well to Fred, and he seemed to get a great deal of traction on the front end. But business has actually declined. Although Bob provided him with a more technical exposure and a deeper dive into the complexities of the services the company provides, Fred appears to be out of his element. Bob is now thinking about reassigning one of his other people to help with some of the technical difficulties the client appears to be experiencing. He has a sinking feeling that Fred might not be able to learn what he needs to know to represent the company in a credible manner.

We all know ascent is fraught with obstacles and dangers: but just getting there isn't enough. Now the question becomes, "How do I stay here long enough to have a lasting positive impact on this place?" To do so, you must build a healthy, viable company that provides growth opportunities for people. You just can't do that with toxic people (see the next chapter). A sad fact of life is that some people choose to do harmful things. But let's talk about good people first.

In *Good to Great*, Jim Collins describes the characteristics of great leaders as being modest and even self-deprecating, yet also as having an unwavering ambition for the company. They never lose faith in ultimate success, but also face facts in a brutally direct manner. One of his adages is that success is a function of getting the right people on the bus and getting them in the right seats.

The leader's ability to select and develop the right people is crucial to the success of any organization. In addition to Collins's "First the *who*, then the *what*", other people as diverse as humorist Leo Rosten ("First rate people hire first rate people, second rate people hire third rate people") and former Secretary of Defense Donald Rumsfeld ("A's hire A's, B's hire C's") emphasize the importance of getting the best people. A leader has no higher duty than choosing people who will ensure the future success of the organization.

What are the characteristics of the right people – those who will be good for your business and help foster a culture of success? Theories of personality can be conflicting and confusing. Some measures of personality lead to typecasting that doesn't hold up when subjected to rigorous predictive analysis. Competency models used by many organizations to define the desirable characteristics of their people are usually too narrow. They can lead managers to look at the wrong things or ignore important aspects of "the whole person" when hiring or developing their people. Competency models don't often differentiate between what can be taught and what could be an ingrained trait or ability. Some things simply can't be changed or developed to any significant extent.

Having personally conducted many thousands of psychological assessments for business organizations, I still sometimes find it difficult to understand and integrate the multifaceted and often conflicting data gathered in the assessment process. The framework described in this chapter, however, has helped me stay focused on the most important factors in assessment and in coaching for development. It can also help you make better selection and development decisions in your own organization.

We can all get better at just about anything. In spite of the fact that there are apparently hardwired traits, abilities, and characteristics, improvement is possible. If we define the right kind of goals, pursue them with the right strategies, and monitor our progress, we can improve. Psychologist Heidi Halvorson has offered compelling evidence for the dynamic nature of human ability in her book *Succeed: How We Can Reach Our Goals.* This is quite encouraging, and has broad implications for self-development, coaching, parenting, and for educational applications. As with anything worthwhile, progress takes insight, planning, time, and effort.

Unfortunately, unless you're running a well-funded early career developmental program, you don't have the resources or time to bring in raw material and nurture it to full potential. If you're a typical recruiter or hiring executive, you need competent people with the talents and skills necessary to hit the battlefield in full stride. A quote attributed to Lewis Pierson, businessman and former president of the US Chamber of Commerce in the early part of last century, describes your situation: "Business is like a man rowing a boat upstream. He has no choice; he must go ahead or he will go back." If that was true nearly one hundred years ago, it's certainly so now.

This is not to downplay the importance of good management and leadership practices; but unless you're hiring for entry-level jobs, you simply don't have the luxury of providing the long-term nurturance, coaching, care and feeding of new hires necessary to develop them to full potential. At least, not in the timeframes you face. Although people have great capacity for improvement and development, for your purposes, your candidates typically need to look more like the finished product than a work-in-progress on certain key factors. They must bring with them the appropriate traits and aptitudes that enable them to learn, adjust, and make a contribution, in relatively short order.

The necessary business skills can be learned relatively easily and quickly. It takes more time to move the needle on these more deeply ingrained qualities. Long-term and enduring patterns of behavior are traits. An old nugget of business wisdom is "Hire for trait, train for skill." But if certain traits aren't in place, some skills won't develop, no matter how hard one tries. To hire or promote the best people who can quickly become assets in our organizations, we must act as if some things are innate.

In previous writings, I have described the *I-Competencies*: the Intellectual, Interpersonal, Integrity, and Intensity factors. These characteristics are generally hardwired, at least for the context and timeframes within which a business leader must operate. Think of them as *head, heart, guts* and *will*. These are the foundation competencies: the result of genetics and the values and attitudes one absorbs from early family and societal or cultural influences. They are fundamental, and cannot be developed quickly or significantly by training, coaching, or experience. In this respect, they differ from surface competencies such as formal presentation skills, spreadsheet skills, technical knowledge base, and so forth, which can be taught. Since you cannot change these factors to any significant degree, they should be targeted in your selection process.

The I-Competencies

The Intellectual Competency (Head)

This factor has traditionally been measured by standardized tests that predict success in school, but test scores alone aren't enough. The Intellectual Competency, or general intelligence, encompasses mental agility, quickness and creativity, depth of knowledge, logical reasoning, and common sense. This factor is a combination of people's unique mix of skills and abilities: and how well they use them to solve problems. People who make smart decisions and who use their talents effectively are more successful over time than those who make bad decisions or squander their intellectual resources. After almost one hundred years of scientific research on this dimension, the results are quite clear and unambiguous. This is the best predictor of job performance available. There are always exceptions to the rule: there are very bright people who never amount to anything and there are people of rather average intelligence who work hard and achieve great things. But the correlation between this competency and performance over time is clear and consistent across jobs and occupations. In the story introducing this chapter, Bob deals with the consequences of hiring someone who is not strong enough in this competency into an analytically demanding role.

The Interpersonal Competency (Heart)

No matter how clever you are, and how elegant or elaborate your problem solutions, if you can't communicate them to others and convince others of their merits, it doesn't matter. People who have good social skills and who get along with other people are much more successful as a group than those who don't have as many talents in this area. They have greater influence in the group because others like them and feel good about them. The Interpersonal Competency is the key that unlocks the door of influence. It enables you to communicate the worth of your ideas. This competency includes general social and persuasive skills, social insight and intuition, likeability and persuasiveness. The Intellectual Competency enables you to solve the problem. The Interpersonal Competency enables you to convince other people that your solution is a good one.

The Integrity Competency (Guts)

This is broader than just the basic honesty-dishonesty dimension, although that's a fundamental. This competency is the cornerstone of building trust, one of the primary factors of credibility. It includes general conscientiousness, discipline, and follow-through. People with high integrity meet their commitments within the timeframes agreed upon, and according to standards expected, and let everyone know in plenty of time if the commitment can't be met. Part of this competency includes the ability to focus, and to use your talents and aptitudes with appropriate discipline. This factor holds things together and facilitates trust and consistency of performance. The greater the perceived integrity, the greater the trust.

The Intensity Competency (Will)

This is the motivation factor. It includes energy, stamina, drive, and the ability to get fully engaged. People with high intensity are active, not passive. They are driven by a need to get things done and to see results. With proper control and focus, people with high intensity achieve at higher levels than those with only average amounts of stamina and energy. This is the fuel that provides force for achieving goals, and for staying motivated in the face of obstacles. It is often referred to as general drive or motivation. The more motivated you are, the more likely you are to achieve results, and consequently the greater your ability to influence others by virtue of your accomplishments and general credibility.

KEY CONCEPTS

Although everyone can improve, some things take too long to change enough to make a difference in the business context and timeframe. Therefore, we must select people for specific fundamental and stable traits and aptitudes. These are foundation competencies:

intellectual, interpersonal, integrity and intensity. These "I-Competencies" can be thought of as head, heart, guts, and will.

EIGHT

Protecting your organization
from the wrong people

On her way to a promising job interview, Maria can't help feeling a sense of loss and disappointment when she thinks about some of the reasons she is seeking a change. When she joined her current organization, a nonprofit dedicated to improving local communities, she was enthusiastic and convinced that she could make a real difference. She believed in the mission and she enjoyed the work. The organization has a great reputation and she was proud to be associated with it. Then things began to fall apart, a year or so after her arrival. Her boss hired a new person, a relative of another section head, who started to make trouble immediately. Maria was amazed that no one in authority seemed to notice, or if they did, that they didn't care. The new person immediately took credit for the work of others, and immediately started to gossip and trash coworkers. Although everyone in the unit realized she was bad news, they still had to deal with her. Eventually, this began to sap the energy and motivation of the team, and Maria noticed that people were becoming less and less open and trusting with one another. What had been a great and well-functioning team just a few months before had now become a somber, suspicious, and generally dysfunctional group. She was saddened to see how much of a toxic effect one person could have on a great organization. However, since no one in authority seemed particularly bothered by it, she realized there was nothing she could do. She decided to look elsewhere, and it hasn't surprised her to find that several coworkers are doing the same.

While Jim Collins emphasizes getting the right people on the bus, corporate transformation expert Bob Miles notes that if you get the bus moving in the right direction, the wrong people will get off. Which brings us to the question, "What do the wrong people look like?"

Individual characteristics to avoid

This is simple and important: don't hire bad apples. If you already have them, get rid of them as quickly as possible. One toxic person can do more damage to an executive team than all your star performers can overcome. A few incompetent or lazy team members can ruin the team. In an article describing the *bad apple syndrome*, researchers Will Felps, Terrence Mitchell, and Eliza Byington observed, "The bad is stronger than the good." In one study, they found that just one abrasive or lazy person on the team could bring down the overall performance by 30% to 40%.

Stanford professors Jeffrey Pfeffer and Charles O'Reilly report that leaders who tolerate their high-performing but toxic superstars underestimate the damage they do. For example, they note that one company reluctantly fired their best salesman because he was a jerk with a negative effect on coworkers. Subsequently, none of the other salespeople sold as much as he had as an individual, but the total sales of store increased by more than 25%. The lesson here is that a bad apple can suppress the efforts of others, and that by removing that individual, the other team members begin to thrive.

Allowing abrasive or ineffective people to remain in place sends the message that you are too timid to confront the issue, that you are out of touch, or that you don't care.

Some, if not most, of the causes of poor performance can be related directly to problems with the I-Competencies described earlier. Although all types of ineffective people have a detrimental effect on team performance, a particular category of bad apple deserves special attention. Certain pathological people can do more than just damage internal morale and performance. These people are most likely to get into ethical difficulties. If they're at an executive level, they can do real damage to the organization, up to and including destroying it. The rest of this discussion will focus on them.

There are measures to diagnose some of the pathologies likely to be associated with wrongdoing, but they're not very useful with an executive population. The professional roadmap for clinical pathology definition is the *Diagnostic and Statistical Manual of Mental Disorders (DSM)*, published by the American Psychiatric Association. It's unlikely, however, to see obvious signs of the pathologies described in this work in a normal population, especially a high-functioning group such as managers and executives. While we might see hints of certain pathologies, if they were blatant enough to meet the diagnostic criteria, any person displaying them would be selected out of the process long before arriving as a candidate. In addition, the measures to diagnose these pathologies are typically quite apparent to a normal job applicant. However, although they can be sub-clinical, the expression of milder forms of these pathologies can be related to organizational malfunctions in general, and ethical problems in particular.

Assumptions about world: underlying mechanisms of pathology

When people see the world as a hostile place, and assume others will hurt them if they can, their responses to most life situations are very different from those of normal people. Normal people define reasonable behavior by the cultural norms and standards they have internalized from parental, school, and societal influences. Normal people have a hard time understanding why some people behave poorly – not only being overtly violent, but also acting in more subtle aggressive ways, some of which are readily observable in organizations.

People who see life through the distorted lens of aggression think their pathological actions are reasonable responses to a hostile world. Where normal people see others in a positive light, pathologically aggressive people see them either as weak players to be used or despised, or as strong competitors who pose a threat. They see life as a struggle between dominance and victimization, and believe that aggression is better than cooperation, because cooperation indicates weakness. When given a choice, they prefer force, competition, and displays of power to avoid having others take advantage of them.

Aggressive people are always vigilant for hostile intent and see it where none exists. They misinterpret positive overtures from coworkers as hostile attempts to find and exploit their weaknesses or steal their work. This sets up a vicious cycle – their behavior turns others away from them, and causes defensive reactions: reinforcing their worldview.

They have a keen sense of injustice and are motivated by a desire to get even for perceived wrongs. They seek retribution. When given well-meant and innocent critique, they respond both with anger at the "injustice", and with feelings of inadequacy, a powerful combination that drives negative, hostile behavior. At its worst, this can trigger workplace violence. However, the effects of this aggressive response bias can be seen in theft, sabotage, cheating, malicious gossip, and other negative acts. Aggressive personalities always try to get even, and can always justify their behavior. They are not likely to be swayed by moral arguments.

The pathologically aggressive person operates with very different assumptions. His reasoning is designed to justify and rationalize behavior that harms others. These people are unconcerned with traditional ideas of ethical and moral behavior.

Aggressive personalities can do great damage to a company, especially if they have the veneer of social polish, above average intelligence, and impressive educational credentials. In positions of executive leadership, they can take the company down. However, if we can understand their assumptions, which are beneath their level of awareness, we can avoid bringing these potentially destructive people into our organizations. This is difficult, but there is promising research that could eventually provide some help here. Psychologists Larry James and Mike McIntyre have developed an instrument which appears to be a test of reasoning, but which is in fact a measure of aggressive versus normal assumptions. This measure is not correlated with general intelligence, so pairing it with cognitive tests should be a powerful method to screen for potential pathology. Brighter people with a more normal (that is, less aggressive) worldview are always better hires.

This mechanism is at the heart of many ethical problems. The aggressive worldview can be changed over time if the individual truly understands how harmful it is to him and is truly motivated to change, but this is not an easy task. Moreover, it's beyond the mission scope of most organizations. If you're running a business, you need to keep pathologically aggressive people out of the hiring pipeline.

The aggressive worldview is implicated in the factors

of the *Dark Triad* of pathology: Machiavellianism, psychopathy and narcissism. These are separate but overlapping disorders, all of which generally predict bad behavior. As an upper level graduate student explained, when I was just learning about such stuff, the main thing you need to know about these people is that "They don't care about you!" All three types are characterized by self-centeredness and manipulation. A key factor to remember here is that these disorders are long-term, stable, and resistant to change. They have a strong and consistent influence on the person's behavior over time, and in a wide range of circumstances. Clinical efforts to change such people have not been effective, and in some cases have made things worse. In short, you don't want them in your organization.

The Dark Triad

Machiavellianism
Nicolo Machiavelli, a Florentine poet, musician, playwright, and keen observer of political power, is best remembered for *The Prince*, a biting but accurate treatise on the practical application of power in politics. Although some of his advice is harsh, such as his dictum: "If you must fight, don't wound your enemies ... kill them, their families and friends, so they can't come back to do you harm later"; his messages still carry a certain resonance of uncomfortable accuracy.

Machiavellianism, as a negative term, became one

focus of research in social psychology in the seventies. It was defined as the proclivity to manipulate and exploit using power, intimidation, charm, or other such methods to win personal or organizational advantage. Psychologists Richard Christie and Florence Geis developed a scale to measure a person's level of Machiavellianism. People with high scores on this measure are seen as calculating, detached, manipulative, deceptive, and self-centered. They employ all means available to them to get their way; but some of these characteristics are also correlated with rising to power in organizations and, as Machiavelli observed, maintaining power. Those who achieve low scores on the Machiavellianism measure developed by Christie and Geis are usually more empathic, sympathetic, open, and agreeable.

Unfortunately, this measure of potential pathology isn't very useful in helping select people in business organizations, because it is rather transparent. That is, a reasonably bright candidate can easily figure out the right answer. It doesn't take much to understand that the socially acceptable response to such items as "Most people are basically good and kind," or "There's no excuse for lying" is agreement. So, we have to rely on more indirect means.

For instance, high Machiavellianism tendencies are related to low scores on the standard personality factors of agreeableness and conscientiousness (stay tuned for more on this).

Narcissism

In mythology, Narcissus was a handsome young man who eventually fell in love with his own reflection in a pool of water. Freud saw narcissism as the quality of being self-absorbed to the point of pathology. Narcissistic personalities are characterized by an inflated self-concept and self-centeredness in general. They lack empathy for others and typically assume that they are entitled. Their view of themselves is grandiose. They are sometimes flamboyant and have an undeserved and unrealistic sense of superiority.

It's easy to see how people with these characteristics can be destructive to an organizational culture. In their less pathological form, some narcissistic characteristics can help people rise quickly in an organization; but in the long term, their self-centered, superficial, and manipulative characteristics do turn people against them.

Psychopathy

Psychopathy and sociopathy are related terms, sometimes now referred to as antisocial personality disorder. As with other such disorders, they are deep-seated and quite resistant to change. Psychopathy is characterized by lack of concern for others, disregard for social norms, low tolerance for frustration, and a keen ability to rationalize problems by finding blame elsewhere. Psychopaths do not experience guilt, and consequently don't learn much from punishment. They are thrill seeking and impulsive. The worst cases of psychopathy rarely make it to the executive suite, because their anti-social behaviors usually serve to remove them from the path for succession and progression in most organizations. However, as with Machiavellianism, milder and more attenuated expressions of their deeper nature can sometimes give them a competitive advantage. A charming psychopath can do a great deal of damage in an organization, especially if he or she is brighter than average.

Other individual factors related to organizational dysfunction

Locus of Control

Locus of control, a concept first defined and researched by psychologist Julian Rotter, refers to the belief that we control our lives by our own actions (*internals*) or that we're mostly at the whim of outside forces (*externals*). Note that this has nothing to do with the normal personality traits of introversion or extraversion that will be discussed a little later.

Internally-controlled people are more satisfied with their jobs, have a more favorable attitude towards their managers, and feel better about salary increases and career advancement. They see themselves as more in charge of their own destiny and as responsible for their own actions. They are less likely to succumb to negative peer pressure. When motivated by positive factors, they have a strong moral compass.

Externally-controlled people are likely to believe more in luck and happenstance than in their own ability to make things happen. They feel that their own efforts do not significantly affect outcomes. They are more likely to see themselves as victims and, because of this, more likely to justify "getting even" thinking, which leads to bad behavior.

We can measure this factor, but as with Machiavellianism, the test for it is easy to manipulate. Rotter's original IE scale, if applied to a work environment, would have candidates indicate whether they agree or disagree with such statements as "Promotions come to those who do a good job." Most people would rightly assume that if you want the job, you should agree with these types of statements. If using such a test as a selection tool, you're selecting for higher intelligence, but perhaps not much else. For selection purposes, the methods to estimate this characteristic must be more subtle than tests that have been used for research on it. Moreover, because most people in executive ranks score in the internal control direction anyway, it would not be particularly useful.

Cognitive Moral Development (CMD)

A helpful framework through which to view moral and ethical decision-making is offered by psychologist James Rest. His model describes four basic components of moral decision-making: identifying it as a moral issue; making a moral judgment about it; focusing on how to deal with it;

and taking the appropriate action. This model makes use of the developmental stage framework for moral reasoning suggested by psychologist Lawrence Kohlberg. He outlined six stages, from Stage One (recognition only of oneself, the perspective of the infant) to Stage Six (recognition and adherence to universal ethical principles) as the basis for ethical behavior. People who have reached the higher stages of CMD make better ethical decisions.

The traditional way to measure this factor is to present a scenario with a dilemma of competing values, such as determining the rightness or wrongness of stealing something from someone who owns it, to help someone whose life depends on getting it. This is cumbersome in a selection situation, and of questionable value, because it is more of a surface competency. That is, people can learn to think differently about complex issues when given the proper training and perspective. Therefore, ethical decision-making is better addressed in training than used as a selection factor, unless there are blatantly obvious signs of problems. If you're selecting for intelligence, you also indirectly help to increase the overall cognitive moral development of the organization, because brighter people are able to understand the subtleties of ethical issues more readily than those who aren't as gifted, *as long as they have the proper instruction.* Remember, select for the foundation competency (the Intellectual Competency, in this case) and train for the surface competency (CMD).

KEY CONCEPTS

Just a few bad apples will spoil any team. Left unchecked, they can wreck a good corporate culture. Get rid of lazy, incompetent, or toxic people. Better yet, don't hire them in the first place. Just as there are consistent characteristics of good people, there are also consistent characteristics of people who can harm an organization. These include the "dark triad" of pathology – Machiavellianism, psychopathy and narcissism. These factors are related to a general inclination towards aggression. People who have a sense of personal control over their environment and people who can understand some of the subtleties of ethical decisions make better employees.

Active Leadership

NINE

How to get the people you want: selection tools and techniques

Arthur has been tapped for a special project. His company has grown through acquisitions but has not always done a great job of integrating them. Many of the policies, procedures and systems are inconsistent. He has been chosen to focus on the process of selecting good people for the newly expanded company. His law degree and recent work in the general counsel's office have given him a good base of knowledge of employment law and the various pitfalls associated with selection. However, this makes the job more frustrating because the procedures of the various new divisions are all over the map. He wants to avoid the typical "department of prevention" HR reputation, but he needs to protect the organization and, in some cases, to protect the general managers from themselves. To make it even more difficult, it's hard to find a good source of best practices. Some organizations swear by extensive testing while some avoid testing altogether. Some do background checks, some do drug screens, some do panel interviews and some appear to be completely haphazard. Although he's excited by the opportunity and realizes that this is a great chance to make a real contribution, he's not looking forward to the political battles he'll have to fight to develop a robust system and to get the field to accept it.

Of course, the best way to avoid problems with the wrong people is not to hire them in the first place: and of course a few will always slip through the cracks, no matter how good your process. However, an effective selection system enables you to narrow the margin for error, and to avoid many headaches.

Be extra careful when you feel the heat to hire someone quickly. The adage "Hire in haste, repent at leisure" is painfully true. Peter Drucker observed that crooks rise to the top in boom times. When a company is growing and experiencing great success, the controls usually aren't in place to keep the bad actors from being hired or promoted into positions from which they can do real damage. He also noted that the most crucial promotions are those into the group from which tomorrow's leaders will be selected. Be sure you know what message is being sent when you promote someone, and make sure your pipeline for future executives is filled with only the best people. It's better not to hire someone, even if it might limit your ability to take advantage of fleeting opportunities, than to hire the wrong person.

Naturally, your selection system should include any position- or company-specific knowledge or skills, but it should also include the broader I-Competency framework. And it should be especially tailored to screen for the characteristics associated with good ethical decisions, and to reject those candidates who have the characteristics associated with bad ones. All other things being equal, people who make better ethical decisions are brighter than average, more conscientious, and less self-centered.

There is no substitute for a valid, fair, and rigorous selection system to help an organization become successful over time. Such systems consist of an active pipeline of diverse and appropriate recruits, a structured screening process, and rational decision-making applied consistently. Any selection system must also be validated according to legal and professional guidelines, and must be administered fairly.

Testing programs

Testing is often a part of the selection system, especially for entry-level jobs. The different types of tests include integrity testing, personality inventories, cognitive tests (which include reasoning, math skills, and vocabulary), role-plays (such as inbox assessments), skills testing (such as programming language proficiency), physical abilities tests, and many others. Testing is most defensible when used to measure factors that have been determined by appropriately rigorous statistical procedures to have an impact on successful job performance.

A cornerstone of good testing programs is the job analysis, a structured process which defines the success factors for the position under consideration. However, the job analysis is typically most useful for lower level positions, where the competencies are clear and simple. It's more difficult to define a limited and tightly delineated set of competencies for managerial and executive level positions. In these cases, we rely more on the broader foundational *I-Competencies*, which are best gleaned by a full psychological assessment.

The types of tests generally used to help make selection decisions are described below; but no matter what sort of test you use, be sure to validate it for your environment. That is, it should predict performance and shouldn't discriminate on anything other than performance.

Integrity tests

Integrity tests would seem to be a natural, if you want to select people who will help build an ethical culture. However, integrity tests can be rather intrusive and objectionable. They're useful in narrowing the focus on people who are less likely to steal, but they're typically pitched at a low level. If your company must deal with large inventories, multiple cash transactions, or other situations in which a person is likely to be tempted, they could be helpful. They're not appropriate, however, for managerial and executive level people in most circumstances. Of course, they give the message that you want to hire only honest people, but they also suggest that you believe most people are dishonest. Most integrity tests have a somewhat punitive feel to them. This probably isn't what you want to communicate right out of the gate, if you're interested in building an atmosphere of trust.

Personality inventories

Personality inventories can help to narrow the margin for error as far as culture fit and fit with a particular job are concerned; but they must be handled with care and sensitivity. You can find many personality tests online that claim to measure all sorts of attributes, but which in reality would be worthless – or get you in trouble – if you used them for selection. These sorts of instruments are sometimes useful for self-insight, but are clearly inappropriate for selection.

Clinical psychologists have developed a variety of measures to assess a wide range of pathologies, including some of the factors implicated in bad ethical decisions. The Minnesota Multiphasic Personality Inventory (MMPI) is the oldest and best researched of these. However, there are two reasons it shouldn't be used for typical business purposes. First, it's intrusive, and contains a number of questions that are inappropriate for a business setting. There have been successful lawsuits filed in response to its indiscriminate and ill-considered use. Second, this instrument is generally considered as a medical test, and is therefore subject to the guidelines and restrictions of the Americans with Disabilities Act (ADA). Personality inventories used to describe normal people aren't restricted by the ADA.

Personality inventories are widely used and often misused. They can be quite helpful, but they should only be used together with many other data points, and should be validated carefully in your environment. At lower levels, ensure you can justify their use by showing how they are related to success on the job. At higher levels, you might be able to gain useful insights for culture fit questions, but they're not perfect and should be used with care and caution.

A widely referenced and scientifically validated model of personality is the *Five Factor Theory* (often referred to as the "Big Five"). These five major factors of personality, measured by many present-day instruments, are described below.

Extraversion

This is a well-researched personality factor. At the most basic level, this is the orientation towards the *external* world of people, things and events ... or towards the *internal* world of thoughts, feelings and ideas. As previously noted, this is *not* the same thing as the Locus of Control concept of internal versus external control discussed earlier. A large component of extraversion is the need for social contact versus a preference for solitary pursuits. People with high scores on this measure are typically sociable, gregarious, extraverted, group-oriented, and expressive. They are not perceived to be quiet, low key or shy. Low scores are often indicative of a mild, reserved, and relatively unexpressive social style; while people with high scores can be overly gregarious and might not know when to back off. This is a major component of the Interpersonal Competency.

Emotional Reactivity

This factor reflects the tendency to be tense, anxious, emotional, or high strung. Some researchers call this factor *neuroticism*. Business people typically score more strongly in the direction of psychological stability and emotional adjustment than do people in the general population. A high score on the emotional reactivity measure doesn't necessarily indicate pathology, but could indicate stress-proneness or volatility under pressure. It could also be a sign that the person is undergoing a particularly upsetting or anxiety-provoking experience.

Unusually low scores can be indicative of a flat, unresponsive, or passive nature. High anxiety can be associated with bad decisions, some of which could be ethical in nature. But psychopaths are known to have low scores on measures of anxiety. This is a component of the Intensity competency, but extremely high or low scores here can have an impact on all of the other competencies.

Behavioral Control

This dimension is related to discipline, focus, tenacity, organization, and conscientiousness. High scorers tend to control their expressions of feeling and emotion, and tend to be attuned to rules and structure. They often feel a keen sense of duty and responsibility. They describe themselves in terms such as conscientious, tenacious, stubborn, inflexible, and controlled. People with extremely high scores might be rigid and inflexible. Low scorers tend to be spontaneous, adaptable, undisciplined, careless, and not detail-oriented. Very low scores can indicate a lack of discipline and organization. Low conscientiousness is correlated with Machiavellianism, but it does not always indicate pathology. This is part of the Integrity Competency.

Agreeableness
People scoring high on this factor are likely to get along with others and to maintain harmonious relationships. They typically describe themselves as cooperative, likable, approachable, softhearted, and easygoing. They are not usually seen as blunt, intense, driven, abrupt, or direct. Very high scores can be associated with passivity and a tendency to value harmonious relationships over task accomplishment. Unusually low scores don't necessarily mean that the person is disagreeable, but they do suggest an intense, demanding, and insensitive style. Low agreeableness is associated with bad ethical decisions, but many very effective leaders have relatively low scores here, so it is not a consistent predictor of problems in and of itself. Agreeableness is a component of the Interpersonal and Intensity Competencies. Low scores on agreeableness have also been implicated in Machiavellianism, narcissism and psychopathy, but the relationship is far from perfect.

Complexity
This factor is related to intellectual curiosity, openness to

information, independence of thought, and the ability to keep long-term objectives in mind. It is often referred to as openness to experience. Along with general intelligence, it is a major part of the Intellectual Competency. High scorers are usually seen as strategic, freethinking, reflective, imaginative, unconventional and intellectual. They are not typically described as tactical, complacent, or apathetic. Low scorers tend to be hands-on, to have focused interests, and to have little inclination towards intellectual or academic issues. Very low scores could indicate a lack of imagination and/or of academic aptitude, while very high scores are sometimes seen in people who are overly theoretical, conceptual, or academic. Complexity is correlated with measures of intelligence, but certainly not a perfect prediction of it.

Cognitive tests

As mentioned in the earlier discussion, the Intellectual Competency is central to effective performance in complex roles. General mental ability is typically the best predictor of performance in an exceptionally wide range of jobs; and cognitive tests hold promise for selection of people who make good decisions. Since Cognitive Moral Development is correlated with intelligence (cognitive aptitude), it stands to reason that brighter people are better able to solve challenging problems, while taking into consideration some of the complexities associated with high-level moral reasoning. However, cognitive tests should be carefully validated and shown to relate to actual job performance in your environment.

Psychological assessment

Testing alone isn't enough to answer many of the subtle but important questions about behavior in the executive suite. A psychological assessment conducted by an appropriately experienced and credentialed professional can provide insights that would be difficult to gain by other selection methods. A full psychological assessment makes use of data from behavioral observation in the interview; an evaluation of the candidate's background, educational and work experiences; and an in-depth analysis of the person's performance on a variety of tests, surveys, and psychometric instruments. This combination of data sources provides a powerful and effective way of looking under the hood. When the assessment is conducted properly, candidates are offered developmental feedback from the process. They often view it as a positive step to help ensure a good fit from both the individual and company standpoints. Not only does it provide the advantage of a much larger arsenal of instruments and data-gathering techniques, but also provides an objective evaluation from an impartial outside observer.

The psychological assessment is a proven and effective tool for candidate selection and for developmental coaching. It is based on research and statistical analysis; but it also incorporates the human intuitive dimension into the assessment process. To be most effective, the assessor should gather post-assessment performance and ROI data to make sure the techniques and methodologies employed are valid and predictive. When used properly, it can help minimize employment mistakes and can help people on the job reach their potential.

The realistic job preview

The realistic job preview is a great way to determine the goodness-of-fit between the person and the position. In fact, this is one of the best ways to do so if you can structure it appropriately. Not only does it give the person a good sense of what daily life in the organization would be like, thereby minimizing potential surprises, it can give hiring managers and potential coworkers a real-world behavioral example of what it would be like to work with that person.

This is an effective method to get beyond the façade of the interview behavior, and the sometimes-undeserved halo of credentials. If you can bring the candidate in for a short period to work on a real-world project, you can learn a lot about the person's technical and interpersonal skills on the job. Structure it as a mini consulting gig, with an appropriate fee for the work. This gives you a chance to evaluate the candidate according to whatever standards, skills, or aptitudes are important for success on the job, as well as to assess that person as far as general interpersonal and cultural fit are concerned.

The cornerstone: the structured behavioral interview

One of the first steps in building a robust and defensible selection system is to teach your hiring managers how to conduct a suitable structured behavioral interview (SBI). They should take selection interviewing seriously, and see it as a crucial part of their jobs. Although Human Resources should be a central component in the process, the field manager shouldn't abdicate responsibility for selection decisions to HR.

The SBI is a best practice solution for selection assessment. It can be used to assess specific competencies, as well as the broader, more fundamental I-Competencies. At its most basic, the SBI is a technique that allows the candidate to describe how he or she has previously handled problems similar to those likely to be encountered in the job under consideration. The most typical type of question takes the form of "Tell me about a time ..." For instance, if you have determined that conflict management skills are a requirement for the role, you would use questions or probes such as the following example.

"Conflict is a fact of life in most organizations. Tell me about a time when you had to deal with a significant amount of conflict at work. What were the circumstances? What did you do? What was the outcome? What would you do differently now? Can you tell me about any other times you've found yourself in conflict with others on the job?"

Notice that the technique involves asking about past

behavior, to include context, actions, and outcomes. As one gains experience with this type of questioning, it becomes easier to evaluate answers to see if, in fact, they do reflect the skill or attribute under investigation.

This is a much more direct way of gathering data than the typically ill-structured job interview, characterized by casual interactions, leading questions, or discussions about things that aren't work related. It's more effective than probing for certain traits you assume are related to success. For instance, encouraging a sales candidate to describe in detail the toughest sale she ever closed and how she did it can tell you a great deal more about the likelihood of her success than knowing that she scores relatively high on extraversion. That might be useful for understanding her, but you must make the intuitive leap that – since extraverts enjoy people – she would be good in sales. The SBI is a more direct and effective way of gathering job-related information.

The SBI process is based on the observation that the best predictor of *future* behavior is *past* behavior in similar circumstances. It can tap into dimensions important to the job, not only specific surface competencies, but also the foundational I-Competencies. It reaches beyond the surface answer, and can improve the consistency of your process by focusing on behavior in previous, similar situations. This helps ensure consistency, fairness, and validity. It can be tailored to specific job or company competencies, and it is easy to learn. It helps to minimize effects of bias and prejudice, and helps an interviewer develop a solid understanding of the job and its relevant competencies.

Background and reference checks

Structured behavioral interviewing, testing programs and psychological assessment can provide a wealth of useful data, but some people can hoodwink any test, psychologist, or interviewer. For a complete and robust screening system, you need more than just a series of interviews and tests or other assessments.

Conduct thorough reference checks and background investigations. This is especially important when you are charmed by the candidate, and feel that such a step would be a waste of time. Psychopaths are skilled at gaining the confidence of others, and bright ones usually do it very well.

Although reference checks typically provide little useful information (because of fears about liability and because candidates rarely provide the names of anyone who might give a questionable reference) they are still occasionally helpful. Sometimes, reference sources can provide you with the names of others with whom the person has worked. In addition, when candidates know you are checking references, they are more likely to be truthful.

At some point in the interview, if you ask something like "When we check your references, what do you think they'll say your major strengths and major needs for improvement are?" it is likely to elicit more thoughtful answers than, "What are your strengths and weaknesses?" The implied warning that you verify interview data typically gets attention.

A good way to obtain information about past behavior is the background check. Be sure, however, that you're in compliance with any local laws that regulate the procedure for informed consent. Always verify education and employment. If the person is going to operate in a significant capacity, or in a position of trust in your organization, you need to know about felony convictions, bankruptcies (both personal and corporate), lawsuits, licensure revocations, and other vital personal and career aspects. Be very careful with candidates who seem to be too good to be true. We're too prone to skim over this important step when we feel especially good about a candidate, and fear we might lose that candidate if we delay. This is usually a big mistake. The old cliché is applicable: Hire in haste, repent at leisure.

KEY CONCEPTS

A good selection system is necessary to help get the right people into the company, and to avoid hiring the wrong people. The best selection systems include complete psychological assessment for high-level positions; appropriate and validated skill, aptitude and personality testing for key jobs; a structured behavioral interview process for all jobs; and effective background and reference checks.

TEN

Organizational culture:
getting the environment right

Deborah has transformed one of the worst performing plants in the company to one of the stars. She appreciated the formal recognition as general manager of the year, but what she enjoys most is knowing she has made a real difference in the organization and in people's lives. Although there was plenty of complexity and heavy lifting involved in the turnaround, she knows that the keys to her success were simple. It didn't take a genius to see that people thought no one cared what happened, and that they were behaving accordingly. Just getting the place cleaned up and painted made a huge difference. The previous GM paid no attention to the appearance of the plant, and spent as little money as possible on what he considered frivolous things such as grounds maintenance and janitorial services. She saw immediately that the overall look and feel of the work environment gave a clear message that it was OK to be sloppy, and that management was not interested in anything but getting the widget out the door.

Her second major change was to hold people accountable. If they did not meet their commitments on time, she gave them direct feedback about her concerns, and made sure they understood that there would be consequences for underperformance in the future. Most people responded well, but there were a few bad apples in the group. She removed them, and was amazed at the positive and visible changes in the attitudes of those who remained. Her acceptance speech for the award was characteristically low-key and self-effacing: "Thank you very much, but this was mostly just a matter of fixing the broken windows."

Characteristics of the organization (the nurture factor)

The previous discussions about the characteristics of people focused on *nature,* or the innate factors a person brings to the organization. You certainly need the right DNA to build an effective organization; but just getting the best people is not enough of a guarantee of success. Now, we shift the focus to *nurture* – the characteristics of the organization that will shape behavior. Cultures reflect unique combinations of personalities and values of their top leaders, and as a result come in a wide variety of flavors. This discussion is focused on two important factors of a successful culture: an environment that fosters ethical behavior; and one that also offers the chance for the growth of its people.

What do we mean by culture? Culture is the shared values, behaviors, and norms of a group. It includes patterns of activities and symbols that give it significance and meaning. Culture, in a business setting, is the essence of *how we do things around here.* Culture is analogous to personality traits. That is, it's stable over time and affects behavior consistently in a wide variety of circumstances. Cultures develop over time, and they can't be changed easily or quickly. However, with consistent attention, motivation, and courage, culture can be re-defined over time. The needle typically moves slowly, but it can be advanced with the right attention, emphasis, and incentives.

Company size and industry type aren't consistently related to ethical culture; but the quality of work experience does seem to be a predictor of good behavior. To the extent that people in the ranks feel a sense of equity, professionalism, and pride in their work, they are inclined to behave well. When they feel their efforts are not rewarded, that their work doesn't make a difference, that others in the company don't care, or that nobody is monitoring their behavior, they're more likely to behave poorly. Still, we need to be careful not to over-regulate. The more onerous the rules, the more likely people are to look for loopholes. This is a tough balancing act.

Involved boards tend to foster better decision-making. Because of this, smaller or private companies benefit from having an engaged and alert advisory board. In my own profession of psychology, most ethics cases brought to the regulating boards involve individual practitioners who work in relative isolation and who don't seek advice from other professionals when potential ethical issues are on the table. Executives need contact with competent colleagues to make sure they're behaving according to appropriate ethical standards and not getting on the slippery slope. People whose decisions are open to scrutiny from others are more likely to make good ones. As H.L. Mencken observes, "Conscience is the inner voice that warns us someone may be looking." An atmosphere of collaboration in the organization helps to increase the chances that good decisions will outnumber bad decisions.

Co-workers

One of our fundamental needs for survival is to figure out what information means, so that we can tell whether it will help or hurt us. One of the best ways to do that is to look to people around us to help interpret that data. As noted in the earlier discussion about influence, the *Law of Social Comparison* explains that people we trust and identify with are a great resource to help make sure we perceive and interpret new data accurately.

We have strong needs to identify with groups we find attractive, or that we feel are powerful, and we tend to take on their ideas and behaviors without conscious effort or questioning. This is also the mechanism behind cults, delusional beliefs, and mob behavior. It has important implications for building and maintaining a desirable company culture.

As organizations grow, the top executives will have less direct contact with people in the ranks. A top executive's good intentions and messages about the right behavior can be lost among competing messages from the person's peers. The peer reference group exerts great pressure on members to conform to its norms and standards, and the force is even stronger in the absence of authority. Parents become keenly aware of this as they realize that the impact of their teenagers' peer group is greater than their own. In a work environment, the peer group is the strongest source of information about how to behave, so the peer group should be of the highest quality, and should receive the right messages from above.

Implicit messages

If we want to create great cultures, we need to keep in mind what author Malcolm Gladwell refers to as *The Power of Context*. He uses the *Broken Windows* theory of criminologists George Kelling and Catherine Coles for illustration. If a vacant building is left with broken windows, vandals tend to break more windows, then break into the building itself, perhaps to become squatters, lighting fires and wreaking other damage. If trash is allowed to accumulate on a sidewalk, more people begin to dump trash there, and eventually it becomes unsafe to park or walk on that street. The clear message given by these environments is that nobody cares and nobody is looking. We hope that people of good character would intervene, but that doesn't happen. In fact, the research shows that the context of the situation is a powerful influence on behavior, regardless of personality characteristics.

Almost ninety years ago, human development researchers Hugh Hartshorne and Mark May conducted a series of classic experiments about character, clearly demonstrating that almost everyone would cheat given the right set of circumstances. They also found that preaching about it had no real effect. Somewhat later, psychologists Phillip Zimbardo and Stanley Milrgam showed that the frightening behavior of seemingly normal people in situations that pull for bad behavior (for instance, under the Nazi regime) is reproducible in the laboratory. Good people can be made to do bad things more easily than we want to believe. We might not want to hear this, but it can't be ignored.

Although recruiting the right people is a fundamental key to building the right kind of organization, we need to remember what psychologists call the *Fundamental Attribution Error*, which refers to our tendency to overestimate the importance of fundamental traits and characteristics, and underestimate the importance of the context and situation. A bad system can corrupt or run off even the best people. Remember: bad is stronger than good.

The good news is that the *broken windows effect* can be reversed. If the environment is cleaned up (graffiti erased, broken windows fixed, trash collected) and if minor transgressions such as turnstile jumping in subway stations are prosecuted, the message changes. The application of this theory is at least partially credited with the dramatic crime reduction in New York City in the nineties. By changing the environmental context in this manner, the message now becomes, "we care, we're watching, and we'll take action." The result is that people behave accordingly. Context is as important as character when it comes to organizational culture. Not only do you need the right people: you need to be sure they're getting the right messages, and that the incentives for positive behavior and sanctions against negative behavior are clear, effective and enforceable.

Leaders

You can't police a culture into becoming what you want, but you can provide the right examples and incentives to produce behavior you want. This is not something that can be delegated. As with most successful initiatives, culture change must start at the top. A company's culture is a reflection of the CEO and top executive team. They must serve as clear role models and remain above reproach. Although an individual's peer group in any organization has great influence on behavior, specific messages from the top are heard loud and clear. The executive team must always stay aware of the *Executive Amplifier* noted in an earlier discussion – all messages, whether intended or not, are amplified and often distorted throughout the organization. And you're *always* sending a message. Unfortunately, bad news gets attention. Furthermore, reports of bad behavior get around more quickly and have greater impact than those of good behavior. The CEO must invest time to coach a team to do the things necessary to develop a different culture. It takes careful investment of time and money. Although culture changes slowly, it *does* change over time if you reinforce the right behavior.

A top executive needs accurate data and knowledge to make good decisions, but leaders tend to get isolated. To build strong and effective cultures, leaders need to seek out dissenting opinions and tolerate bad news. The best of them will face facts unflinchingly and respond accordingly. One of Jim Collins's findings from the *Built to Last/Good to Great* studies is that the most effective leaders build a culture of consistently "confronting the brutal facts." Along these lines, psychologist Carl Rogers' wisdom is worth repeating here: "The facts are always friendly." When you're at the top, there are many ways for information to become garbled or spun by political agendas. The culture of the yes-man is one of cover-up and selective information sharing, which can easily lead to ethical problems for the company. You must be able to handle reality.

How to build a strong culture: getting the context right and fixing problems

Companies can sometimes be successful without a clear vision, but a good mission and values statement can help people keep their efforts focused and can support them to make the appropriate decisions in the absence of specific leadership direction. Companies are better off in general with some definition of their purpose and values, but if it doesn't help people on the shop floor make decisions and execute their work in the proper manner, it's mostly a waste time.

A mission, values and vision statement has the advantage of delivering the right message to the troops, and can help create a shared sense of purpose. But your assumptions must be explicit. It's a good practice to publish a short and clear (that is, not legalistic or ponderous) code of ethics. It should be written by the CEO, with company lawyers checking for legality and precedent, not written by the lawyers and presented to the CEO.

Aside from developing and publishing clear vision, values, and code-of-ethics statements, the following suggestions can help build the culture you want.

- Fix the broken windows. If there are ethical lapses, take care of them. Don't tolerate bad actors simply because they make their numbers.
- Make sure everyone reads and understands the code of ethics. It's not enough just to have a code. You need to be sure all of your people understand the code, and grasp how its concepts apply.
- Get the incentives right. Naturally, you should reward good behavior, but it's also important to move quickly with transgressions. Remember the *hot stove.*
- A leadership development culture should include not only the selection of the right external candidates, but also a systematic program for early identification of internal people with potential. It's crucial that people who are selected for leadership development possess enough of the foundation competencies to benefit from the attention; but selecting the right

person is only the beginning.

- Sensitize your top executives, not only to your ethical principles, but also to the unanticipated consequences of appearances. They need to manage the optics of their actions to avoid even the slightest whiff of questionable behavior. They need to understand that they're always in a fishbowl, and that they must be clear and bright role models for the right kinds of behaviors. Remember, when we know others might be looking, we're more likely to make better decisions.
- Don't preach – it doesn't work.
- Be visible. Leaders who are out in the organization living the culture in a visible way and reinforcing the right behavior have a huge positive impact.
- Incorporate *how* into your measure of *what,* in your performance appraisal process. If a person consistently achieves strong results but does so with questionable behavior, the company suffers in the long run.
- Pay attention to assignments. Consider them carefully, to broaden the person's scope. Let the employee risk failure, work for a really tough boss, and work in an unfamiliar part of the business. Assign work on cross-functional teams where possible.
- Develop and reward teamwork skills, not just individual accomplishment. Practical and useful teamwork training and insights are rarely taught and reinforced.

- Build a feedback-rich environment. This includes the infrastructure of support and resources: formal and informal tools such as 360 feedback; meaningful performance assessment; and individual coaching to help people act on new insights. Provide your executives with developmental coaching tailored to the person and the situation. Aristotle noted that acquiring virtue is like playing a musical instrument. It requires practice and a teacher.
- Encourage community involvement. Not only does this broaden employees' scope and perspective, but it also allows them to serve as ambassadors for the company.

When highly successful people are asked about the things that were most helpful to their careers, they rarely talk about training, educational opportunities, schools or seminars. Their key learning and developmental experiences were more often frightening and characterized by adversity: such as being dumped into a job where they could fail spectacularly; working for a harsh, demanding or incompetent boss; or working in a new job with no preparation. They also often mention the importance of one or more good mentors and role models.

This brings us back to the original point. A culture starts from the top. People watch what the leaders *do*. It has a much more important influence than what they *say*. If the top executives act like good leaders, others will try to find ways to act like good leaders. If they act badly, their people will also model those behaviors.

KEY CONCEPTS

Organizational culture has a strong influence on behavior. A bad system can bring down even the best people over time. Because of this, it's imperative that leaders build and maintain the kind of culture that fosters the right kind of behavior, leadership development, and overall success. You can't police a culture into what you want it to be, but you can provide the right incentives and examples of appropriate leadership behavior. Culture changes slowly, but it does change with consistent and sustained attention from the top.

ELEVEN

For the CEO

Wrapping up his first year as CEO, Eric feels that he's just beginning to get his feet wet. He expected surprises and for the most part was prepared for them. In general he is pleased with the company results although there's always room for improvement. His board has been cooperative and he has managed to build a few key alliances and supportive relationships with some of the most influential members. But he can't help feel a bit of irritation with their seemingly constant needs for attention and information. It's hard to run the company when your key lieutenants spend most of their time tracking down numbers and compiling reports for the board. It's also irritating that many of the board members have only a superficial understanding of his business and the way it really runs. He could have been much more effective had he not been forced to fight a constant stream of regular fires and a couple of potential major crises this year. And of course the never-ending increases in governmental regulation and "assistance" has been a massive burden and distraction. It's no surprise that he hasn't been able to really reflect on the appropriate strategies to deal with a quickly changing competitive and technological landscape. But it appears that people have accepted him and have been willing to line up and follow his direction. That's been gratifying and certainly made his transition easier. However, he is keenly aware that one or two missteps or bad decisions could have a major impact on his ability to maintain their confidence and to continue to lead effectively. He now realizes Shakespeare's wisdom: "Uneasy lies the head that wears the crown." But overall, it's been a good year and he knew what he was getting into when he signed up. Next year, he plans to get a little closer to the ideal expressed by Chinese philosopher Lao Tze a few thousand years ago:

> *A leader is best when people barely know that he exists, not so good when people obey and acclaim him, worst when they despise him. Fail to honor people, they fail to honor you. But of a good leader, who talks little, when his work is done, his aims fulfilled, they will all say, 'We did this ourselves.'*

Barry Switzer, legendary Oklahoma football coach, is reported to be the source of the quote, "He was born on third base and thinks he hit a triple." Granted, there are people who are born into or who marry into successful business families and wind up running the company. Some of these people are very successful due to their own efforts, but some also remind us of Switzer's quote. And there are some people who are particularly good at getting promoted on the basis of their political skills. But if you've had the interest and taken the time to read this far, you've probably been successful, or will be successful, due in large measure to your own efforts.

As a CEO, you will hopefully find that the rewards are great. You are also likely to find, however, that there are unexpected burdens and unintended consequences akin to those noted in the introductory chapter.

The CEO, more than the other top officers, is always on stage and is always held to a higher standard of behavior. Forget this at your peril. Yes, there is a great deal of adulation and admiration for the person at the top. But there is also suspicion, envy and hostility just beneath the surface. Some CEOs sense this on an intuitive level, and might feel a certain amount of guilt or dread as a result. However, others are blind to it, and believe the flattery and the positive press they get merely for having arrived at the position. But as soon as they stumble, they quickly become aware of the precariousness of public opinion, especially if they've stepped on too many people on the way up.

Karma is a bitch. To make it worse, and as Ayn Rand pointed out, people despise the good for being good. Of course, people who are successful, especially those who succeed due to their own efforts, are copied and admired; but they are also objects of envy and resentment.

In general, CEOs don't fail because of a lack of brain-power, motivation, or sense of vision. It's usually more mundane than that. Of course, the wrong strategy at the wrong time can derail a CEO and the company. But more often it's just lack of execution. And lack of execution can make it look like the strategy was flawed. People who make it to the top office can be tempted to assume their hard work is over. When that becomes the case, they are likely to start trying to protect their position rather than doing real work. At that point, they are in for a rude surprise. The heavy lifting in this case involves making tough decisions: making sure that all commitments are delivered according to promise, building strong executive teams, holding people accountable, and making the numbers. Failure to install the right people in the right jobs, or failure to address people problems quickly enough, creates a certain blueprint for disaster.

Authors Ram Charan and Geoffrey Colvin have studied successful and ineffective CEOs. Their findings about the characteristics of successful top executives, presented in their article *Why CEOs Fail*, echo our earlier observations about the attributes of good people in general (the I-Competencies):

- Integrity, maturity and energy
- Business acumen
- Judgment of people
- Organizational savoir-faire
- General mental ability, intellectual curiosity, and a global mindset
- Great judgment
- An exceptional drive for results and accomplishment
- Strong motivation to grow and to apply new knowledge

So what happens to the lucky (?) few who do make it to the top spot? Be careful what you wish for. Professors Michael Porter, Jay Lorsch and Nitin Nohria summarize their observations on unexpected consequences and surprises when one reaches the top spot in their article, *Seven Surprises for the CEO*. Although their studies are generally focused on public companies, most of these concepts apply across the board. Below is a summary of their observations, and advice on how to handle them.

You can't *run* the company

External pressures and the volume of internal demands are much greater than before. In addition, even though your functional knowledge might have been instrumental in getting you to this position, you can't rely as heavily on it now. You must realize that there are real gaps in your knowledge and expertise, and you have to balance the dual role of Mr. Inside vs. Mr. Outside. Despite the power of the CEO's position, there's often a sense of uselessness or lack of real influence.

You can give orders, but it comes with a high cost

Giving orders ultimately triggers defensiveness and resentment because it erodes the authority of your people. If you must constantly overrule their decisions, that's a sign of your failure to communicate accurately and effectively. Or that you haven't built a competent leadership team.

It's hard to know what's *really* going on

You're bombarded with data, and much of it is unreliable. By the time the information has reached you, it has been filtered to excess.

You're always sending a message
Everything you say and do is scrutinized, analyzed, amplified, and interpreted. Not only that: it's often *mis*interpreted, sometimes drastically.

You can't think out loud anymore
CEOs find that it's very difficult to manage the internal and external constituencies, while giving a consistent and truthful message.

You're not *really* the boss
If you're running a public company, the board has ultimate power. Managing those relationships is a drain, even when they're very good. Even though you thought you'd be calling the shots now, you can't stop managing upwardly. Before, you had only one boss. Now there might be ten or more, most of whom have little real knowledge about your business; but you can't ever let your board members feel uninformed. You need to actively develop and drive the relationships, so you can transform meetings with them into participatory, collaborative discussions rather than show-and-tell sessions.

If you're running a private company, even if you're the sole owner, you still must depend upon many people over whom you have little or no direct control for ultimate success. Another complicating factor is the increasingly onerous regulatory climate, at least in the US. Due to an excessive governmental appetite for control, facilitated by flawed cultures at a few large companies and their (supposed) regulating authority organizations, CEOs and boards now have to deal with such obstacles as Sarbanes-Oxley. The steady stream of new regulations and threats of litigation make boards even more dysfunctional, so conventional board management strategies don't apply as well now as before.

Pleasing the shareholders is not the goal

Shareholders and analysts have a short-term mindset. They come and go. The CEO needs to keep the long term in view. The goal is to create sustainable economic value. High stock prices will eventually collapse without a fundamental competitive advantage, and long-term profitability is what matters.

You're still only human

So don't believe your positive press or other sources of flattery. You simply can't do everything well. This is the most draining job, physically and emotionally, that you'll ever have, and there's no such thing as balance. There are only trade-offs. Your relationships with family and friends will change, so don't get so caught up in your legacy that you lose sight of everything else.

What does this mean to the CEO in his or her daily activities? The implications of these observations offer guidelines for successfully navigating the tricky leadership and political waters that are the stuff of every CEO's life.

First, the CEO must lead by managing organizational context, not day-to-day operations. Many new CEOs feel worthless and powerless – entering the office with a strong pull to *do* something. Being active and involved is what made them successful up to this point. Now their power comes more from the symbolism of their words and behaviors as from their direct efforts to *manage.*

Second, the position doesn't automatically confer the *ability* to lead, nor does it provide a guarantee of loyalty. The power to really lead and transform must be earned, and can be easily lost if the vision isn't convincing or if actions are different from the values espoused. Success depends on the ability to enlist voluntary commitment and make people want to follow you.

The CEO and top executive team set the tone and define the organization's culture and values through words and actions. They demonstrate how to behave.

Finally, failure to recognize you are human, and not omnipotent, results in arrogance, exhaustion, and a short tenure. Take care of business: but also take care of yourself.

KEY CONCEPTS

CEOs typically fail because of a lack of execution, not

because of a lack of vision. The CEO is always on stage, and is always held to a higher standard of behavior. There are sometimes unpleasant surprises at the top, most of which revolve around having less control than anticipated.

In conclusion

Many very bright and competent people don't have the unique combination of motivations, interests, and other necessary characteristics to be happy and effective in an executive role. This seems obvious, but it's not always the case. A major key to success is first to make sure you really want to be the leader, then figure out how good you are at it so you know how to set goals for improvement. Don't be discouraged, however. Remember the findings of Heidi Halvorson referenced earlier – we can improve on just about anything when we set the right goals and apply the right strategies. The United States Marine Corps has clearly shown that people can be taught to be good leaders. Although few of us can be considered "natural leaders", if you *want* to succeed, you *can* succeed. It takes insight, hard work, and good feedback.

Here's a review of some of the key actions that facilitate success in a leadership role:

Define the future

This is basic. You need to know where you're taking your troops, and they need to understand that and support it. We've seen leaders' ratings from their subordinates improve across the board when the only thing they changed in their behavior was to articulate a clear goal that captured the imagination and support of people in the ranks. Paint a vivid picture of a successful future.

Communicate the goal

The obvious is easily overlooked. It does no good to define the goal if people don't know what it is, and what it means for them. The message should be clear and consistent, and you need to be prepared to repeat it often. Understand and use the principles of influence and persuasion. Use stories and analogies to engage them, and make the goal clear and real for them.

Be optimistic but realistic

Make sure the goal is a stretch but reachable. Communicate in an upbeat, positive manner, but don't be a Pollyanna. Answer questions directly and acknowledge a lack of information when necessary. Give clear feedback about progress and performance against the goal, and be sure to reward good performance. Remember the quote by James Baldwin: "Not everything that is faced can be changed. But nothing can be changed until it is faced."

Model openness and trust

Absolute integrity is essential. It is naïve to ignore political dangers, but it would be a disaster to become cynical, or to make decisions based only on your own political gain. Executives live in a world that encourages predatory behavior. Don't neglect political dangers, but set the example of dealing in a straightforward manner. The more consistent and fair you are, the more likely others are to deal with you in the same way.

Seek feedback

You might have a strong game plan, but you need to know where you are before you can know how to get where you want to be. Objective feedback is hard to come by, and if you don't seek it, you usually won't get it. You need to know how your people see you, and what they need from you. Structured methods for upward feedback such as multi-rater or 360-degree ratings are helpful, but not infallible. Ask people who have had a chance to observe you what you do well and what you need to improve on.

Be relentlessly consistent

This consistency should be obvious in your behavior, your integrity, and your willingness to make the hard decisions. If you're heading in the right direction, keep going. Remember that it takes hard work and sustained effort to create the right culture.

Get good people and let them go

Empowerment's fine as a value in general, but if you empower the wrong people, you and your organization are likely to go down the tubes. To make your life easier over time, don't compromise on selection. A's hire A's and B's hire C's. The worst thing you can do with marginal people is to let them operate without structure or direction. The worst thing you can do with good people is to manage them too tightly. Once you know they're good and they're with the program, give them broad goals, then get out of their way until they need help.

Events can conspire against a person on any journey, and being in the wrong place at the wrong time can trump heroic effort. However, if you take the insights and suggestions in this book to heart, and act on them appropriately, you will be a better leader. Use them as a starting blueprint if you're early in your career. If you're further along the journey, reflect on them and see how well they match your own experiences. They might help you maintain perspective and keep the right focus.

I'll end with a beginning. I once saw a great introduction to an executive team developmental off-site, which I shamelessly borrow whenever I have a chance. Apologies to the source, but it was many years ago, and all I remember was how helpful the exercise was to frame the session and get the participants focused on the work they needed to do. My version of it goes something like this:

> Welcome. Let me begin by asking a question. What are your expectations for this session?
>
> Before you answer that, let's look at it a little more closely. *Expectations* imply that you're wishing or hoping to get something. Now let's compare the concept of *expectations* with that of *intentions*. Intentions imply that you'll cause, create, or do something: that you will make

something happen.

Expectations suggest a passive, internally focused, externally controlled – even selfish – mindset. But *intentions* suggest an active, externally focused, internally controlled attitude, and the willingness to take a risk.

Expectations imply a fuzzy vision – you're open to what's coming, and you think you want it, although you might not have defined it. You can't have an intention, however, without knowing what you want – *intentions* imply clear vision.

Expectations reside more in the world of the transactional – you'll get something if you do something; but *intentions* are more transformational – you'll change something if you make the effort.

Expectations are more often associated with managing a process. *Intentions* are more about leading.

So ignore my first question about your expectations. What I really mean to ask is this: what are your *intentions* for this session?

I don't know what expectations you had before starting this book, but what I'd love to know now is ... What are your *intentions*, after having finished? How do you *intend* to apply the principles of active leadership in your journey?

Winston Churchill observed that the price of greatness is responsibility. The cost of self-actualization, which includes meeting your potential as a leader if you have chosen this path, is a keen sense of what *can* be done – and a sometimes painful sense of *how much is still left to do.*

I wish you all the best on your journey.

Bibliography

American Psychiatric Association (1994). *Diagnostic and Statistical Manual of Mental Disorders.* Arlington, VA.

Bass, B. and Stogdill, R. (1990). *Bass & Stogdill's Handbook of Leadership: Theory, Research, and Managerial Applications.* (3rd ed) Free Press.

Belbin, M. (1981). *Management Teams: Why They Succeed or Fail.* Wiley.

Blake, R. and Mouton, J. (1985). *The Managerial Grid III: The Key to Leadership Excellence.* Gulf Publishing.

Bostock, D. (2000). *Aristotle's Ethics.* Oxford: University Press.

Carnegie, D. (1981). *How to Win Friends and Influence People.* (Revised Edition) Pocket Books.

Charan, R. and Colvin, G. (1999). *Why CEOs Fail.* Fortune, June 21.

Christie, R. and Geis, F. (1970). *Studies in Machiavellianism.* Academic Press.

Clance, P. (1985).*The Impostor Phenomenon: When Success Makes You Feel Like a Fake.* Bantam Books.

Collins, J. (2001). *Good to Great: Why Some Companies Make the Leap ... and Others Don't.* HarperBusiness.

Drucker, P. (2004). *The Daily Drucker.* HarperCollins.

Felps, W., Mitchell, T. and Byington, E (2006) *How, When, and Why Bad Apples Spoil the Barrel: Negative Group Members and Dysfunctional Groups.* Research in Organizational Behavior, 27, 175 – 222.

Festinger, L. (1954). *A Theory of Social Comparison Processes.* Human Relations, 7, 117-140.

Fisher, C. (2002). *Corporate Culture and Performance.* Presentation at the Society for Industrial/Organizational Psychology 10th Annual Conference.

Frankl, V. (2006). *Man's Search for Meaning.* Beacon Press.

Gladwell, M. (2000). *The Tipping Point: How Little Things Can Make a Big Difference.* Little Brown.

Golson, H. (2011). *Influence for Impact: Increasing Your Effectiveness in Your Organization.* H Lloyd Publishing.

Greenleaf, R., Spears, L., and Covey, S. (2002). *Servant Leadership: A Journey into the Nature of Legitimate Power and Greatness.* (25th Anniversary Edition) Paulist Press.

Halvorson, H. (2010). *Succeed: How We Can Reach Our Goals.* Hudson Street.

Hartshorne, H. and May, M. (1928-1930). *Studies in the Nature of Character.* Macmillan.

Hersey, P. (1985). *The Situational Leader.* Warner Books.

James, L. and McIntyre, M. (2000). *Conditional Reasoning Test of Aggression Test Manual.* Psychological Corporation.

Jones, T. (1991). *Ethical Decision Making by Individuals in Organizations: An Issue-Contingent Model.* Academy of Management Review, 16, 366-395.

Kelling, G. and Coles, C. (1996). *Fixing Broken Windows: Restoring Order and Reducing Crime in Our Communities.* Free Press.

Kohlberg, L. (1971). *Stages of Moral Development.* Kramer.

Kofman, F. (2006). *Conscious Business: How to Build Value Through Values.* Sounds True.

Machiavelli, N. (1513, reissue 1984). *The Prince.* Bantam Classics.

McCall, M. and Lombardo, M. (1983). *Off the Track: Why*

and How Successful Executives Get Derailed. Center for Creative Leadership.

McCrae, R. and Costa, P. (1987). *Validation of the Five-Factor Model Across Instruments and Observers.* Journal of Personality and Social Psychology, 52, 81–90.

McGregor, D. (1960). *The Human Side of Enterprise.* McGraw Hill.

Miles, R. (1997). *Leading Corporate Transformation: A Blueprint for Business Renewal.* Jossey-Bass.

Milgram, S. (1974). *Obedience to Authority.* Harper & Row.

O'Fallon, M. and Butterfield, K. (2005). *A Review of the Empirical Ethical Decision-Making Literature.* Journal of Business Ethics, 59, 375-413.

Paulhus, D. and Williams, K. (2002). *The Dark Triad of Personality: Narcissism, Machiavellianism and Psychopathy.* Journal of Research in Personality, 36, 556-563.

Pfeffer, J. (2010). *Power: Why Some People Have It – and Others Don't.* Harper Business.

Porter, M., Lorsch, J. and Nohria, N. (2004). *Seven Surprises for the CEO.* Harvard Business Review.

Pressfield, S. (2011). *Do the Work.* The Domino Project.

Rand, A. (1967). *Capitalism: The Unknown Ideal.* Signet.

Rest, J. (1986). *Moral Development: Advances in Research and Theory.* Praeger.

Ross, L. (1977). *The Intuitive Psychologist and His Shortcomings: Distortions in the Attribution Process.* In L. Berkowitz (Ed), *Advances in Experimental Social Psychology,* 10. Academic Press.

Rotter, J. (1966). *Generalized Expectancies for Internal Versus External Control of Reinforcement.* Psychological Monographs, 80, 1-28.

Seligman, M. (1991). *Learned Optimism: How to Change Your Mind and Your Life.* Knopf.

Williams, R., Fadil, P. and Armstrong, R. (2005). *Top Management Team Tenure and Corporate Illegal Activity: The Moderating Influence of Board Size.* Journal of Managerial Issues, XVII, 4, 479-493.

Zimbardo, P. and Ebbeson, P. (1970*). Influencing Attitudes and Changing Behavior.* Addison-Wesley.

Active Leadership

Dr. Golson is a founder and President of Management Psychology Group (MPG), a consultancy of licensed psychologists. His firm specializes in assessment for selection and development, selection system design and validation, leadership coaching and development, and leadership succession facilitation. He has personally conducted over ten thousand psychological assessments for business clients. Early in his career, he was an Army officer and an IBM marketing representative. In addition to MPG, he was a founder of eTest.net, one of the first online testing companies. His professional memberships include the Society for Industrial/Organizational Psychology and the Division of Consulting Psychology of the American Psychological Association. He is certified by the American Board of Professional Psychology (ABPP). He consults with CEOs and top executive teams on issues of leadership team effectiveness, leadership succession, executive selection and unique life-at-the-top questions and problems. He is the author of a variety of articles and white papers, including the book *Influence for Impact.*